STEPHEN HAWKING

FLORENCE NIGHTINGALE

NHS

STORMZY

GREAT BRITONS

50 AMAZING PEOPLE WHO HAVE CALLED BRITAIN HOME

ELIZABETH I

NOOR INAYAT KHAN

ALAN TURING

Written by
IMOGEN RUSSELL
WILLIAMS

Illustrated by
SARA
MULVANNY

nosy crow

First published 2021
by Nosy Crow Ltd
The Crow's Nest,
14 Baden Place, Crosby Row,
London SE1 1YW
www.nosycrow.com

ISBN 978 1 83994 015 6

Nosy Crow and associated logos
are trademarks and/or registered
trademarks of Nosy Crow Ltd.

Text © Imogen Russell Williams 2021
Illustrations © Sara Mulvanny 2021

A CIP catalogue record for this book is available from the British Library.

Printed in China

Papers used by Nosy Crow are made from wood grown in sustainable forests.

135798642

CONTENTS

INTRODUCTION

Whether they were born in Great Britain or chose to make their homes here, thousands of extraordinary Britons have brightened Britain – and the world beyond it – and changed both for the better.

Writers like Mary Shelley, Lemn Sissay and Judith Kerr have made readers imagine incredible things, see the world differently, or hope that one day a tiger might come to tea.

Scientists like Alexander Fleming, Stephen Hawking and Tim Berners-Lee have made discoveries that cured illnesses, allowed us to understand the universe better, or connected people all around the world.

Activists like Emmeline Pankhurst and Malala Yousafzai have fought for women's rights, so that all women can vote in government elections or have access to education.

Musicians like Paul McCartney, Yehudi Menuhin and Stormzy have brought joy, entertainment and inspiration to millions of people with their catchy tunes, expressive melodies, or creative song lyrics.

And the work of Britons like Florence Nightingale – who pioneered modern nursing – and Aneurin Bevan – who founded the National Health Service – has ensured that everyone can be looked after when they become ill.

Great Britain's past is complicated, though, and its history – especially the history of the British Empire – hasn't always been great, just, or a source of pride. In the 16th century, England started to invade other countries, wanting to control them and use their wealth and resources. In the places they invaded, they stole land, crops and other valuable things, and often made the people there live according to beliefs that weren't their own. Sometimes, they even enslaved people who lived in these places, or helped others to enslave them. Some British people became very rich, while many people in these countries were treated cruelly and without respect, and became very poor.

The group of countries that Great Britain ruled over was called the British Empire, and the history of those countries is now tightly woven together with Britain's own. Most nations which were part of the Empire have now become independent again – but we are all still living with the impact of the past.

Some people who became part of the British Empire made their homes in Britain and helped to change things for the better. The Black anti-slavery campaigners Olaudah Equiano and Mary Prince settled in Britain in the 18th and 19th centuries. Both were formerly enslaved people who wrote and published their life stories to help people understand the horrors of the slave trade, which was officially abolished in Britain in 1833.

Many years later, in 1965, activist Paul Stephenson fought successfully to get the first law passed that said Britons of all skin colours must be treated equally. Today, the writer Malorie Blackman's gripping *Noughts and Crosses* books show readers all over the world how racism continues to affect people's lives, both in Britain and elsewhere.

Making this list of 50 Great Britons – and choosing who to include and who to leave out – was very hard, and involved some extremely tough decisions. Some people in history have achieved brilliant things, but have behaved in ways that did harm to others too. Some have created amazing works of art, but have also held harmful beliefs.

Roald Dahl, for example, who is here because of the many brilliant books he wrote for children, had prejudiced beliefs about Jewish people that are hurtful and wrong. Recently, his family acknowledged this difficult contradiction too, and wrote an apology for the harm these views caused.

Winston Churchill is considered one of Britain's greatest prime ministers, but he also held racist beliefs. He said and did some things that hurt people of colour, especially Indian people. As somebody who is half Indian myself, I feel that celebrating Winston Churchill's inspiring wartime work does not wipe out the memory of his other words and deeds.

When we look at these people now, and recognise their great talents and achievements, we also need to recognise their faults, and the ways in which their beliefs and actions were not acceptable, then or now. In this way, we can hope to keep changing things for the better.

And things do keep changing, all the time. This list isn't the same list that would have been made 50 – or maybe even 10 – years ago, and 50 years from now it will probably look different again.

Great Britain may be a small place, but it is rich in languages, cultures and brilliant people from all around the world – and there are many more than 50 Great Britons. The ones you can read about here are just a small selection of the inspiring people who have helped shape the country we know today – activists, authors, scientists, musicians, politicians, entrepreneurs and many more.

Who would you have on *your* list, and why?

ALFRED THE GREAT

During a time of constant upset and invasion, the Anglo-Saxon king Alfred the Great successfully defended his kingdom against the Vikings and made peace with them, and created laws to protect and help his people.

THOUGHTFUL BOY

When Alfred was born, in 849, England wasn't one big country but was split into several different kingdoms. Alfred's father ruled the Anglo-Saxon kingdom of Wessex. Alfred was born in the royal palace in Wantage, now in Oxfordshire. He was the sixth and youngest child of his parents, King Aethelwulf and Queen Osburh.

Although Alfred was a prince, he had four older brothers, so he probably didn't think he would ever rule himself. He later said he never wanted royal power – but he still ended up on the throne!

Alfred was a thoughtful boy who liked books, according to a Welsh monk called Asser who wrote his biography. His mother taught him to love poetry, both in the languages of English and Latin. When Alfred was 12, his mother showed her sons a poetry book with beautifully coloured pictures, promising it to whichever of them could learn all the poems in the book first. Alfred, though he was the youngest, won the competition – and the book!

Alfred also travelled to Rome with his father when he was a child, where he met the Pope. This exciting journey might have made him even more interested in Latin, which he enjoyed studying later in his life.

NORTHUMBRIA

MERCIA

EAST ANGLIA

Alfred's three older brothers, Aethelbald, Aethelberht and Aethelred, all reigned as kings of Wessex before Alfred took the crown.

WESSEX

BATTLING THE VIKINGS

For many years, the Danes had been landing on the coast of England from Scandinavia. Danish Vikings (or explorers) carried out raids and tried to claim land as their own. Just as Alfred's third brother, Aethelred, took the throne in 865, they launched a big attack and took control of the kingdom of East Anglia. Alfred fought side by side with Aethelred to defend their kingdom of Wessex. In 867, Alfred married a woman called Ealhswith, but they didn't have much time to enjoy being husband and wife – the Vikings continued to attack!

In 870, Alfred and Aethelred fought nine battles against the Vikings. They were determined not to let the Danes take over Wessex, the only Anglo-Saxon kingdom that hadn't been invaded. When his brother died in 871, Alfred became king, and continued to hold the Danes back from winning power over the whole of England.

However, in 878, the Vikings, led by their king, Guthrum, came close to victory. They staged a surprise attack, and almost all Alfred's fighters surrendered – except Alfred himself! He lay low in a fort in Somerset and made raids on the Vikings while secretly building up another army.

With his new army, Alfred defeated the Vikings at the Battle of Edington. After this, he talked to Guthrum to find a way of making peace between the two sides. Guthrum signed a peace treaty with Alfred, agreeing to convert to Alfred's religion (Christianity) and change his name to Aethelstan. The agreement said that the Vikings would remain on the eastern side of Britain, in their own lands called the Danelaw.

> *There's a famous story that when Alfred was on the run from the Vikings, he hid in a shepherd's hut. The shepherd's wife asked him to watch the little loaves of bread baking in the ashes of the fire. Distracted, Alfred let them burn – and the angry woman told him off! It may not be true, but it is a good story . . .*

WISE AND BRILLIANT RULER

Now that Alfred didn't have to spend all his time fighting the Danes, he began to focus on some of the other responsibilities of being a ruler. He set up schools and rebuilt monasteries, eager to educate his people and preserve the kingdom's knowledge. He thought that learning to read the English language was especially important – and he personally translated many books from Latin to English! He also made laws to protect his people and to punish those who broke important promises.

But he didn't forget that his kingdom would continue to need defending. He built forts throughout the kingdom and he began to build up a strong navy to guard Wessex from the sea. He still had to fight off occasional attacks from other Danish forces. When he died at the age of 50, in 899, he left behind a kingdom in much better order than the one he had inherited – and he is always remembered as a wise and brilliant ruler, both in peacetime and in war.

> *Alfred is the only English king to have been called "the Great". His son, Edward, ruled Wessex after him – and his grandson, Aethelstan, was the first king ever to rule over the whole of England.*

DAVID ATTENBOROUGH

Have you ever watched a nature documentary? Perhaps it was one of David Attenborough's. Born in 1926, Sir David Attenborough is a famous television broadcaster and natural historian. He is the presenter of some of the most popular and powerful shows ever made about plant and animal life on Planet Earth.

YOUNG EXPLORER

Although he has spent nearly all his life working as a television broadcaster, the television was only invented the year after David was born, so he didn't watch TV as a child. His father was the head of University College Leicester, and David and his brothers, Richard and John, spent their childhoods running wild and exploring the university grounds. David loved science, collecting rocks and finding badger setts and birds' nests – he even made a museum at home to display his finds.

David wasn't afraid to get his hands dirty, catching newts to sell to the university for pocket money (at 3 pence a newt – about £2 today!). He was also keen to explore and take risks – when he was 13, he jumped on his bicycle and cycled all the way to the Lake District to spend three weeks there collecting fossils. His parents had no idea where he was!

A clever and hard-working student, David won a scholarship to study Natural Sciences at Cambridge University, and joined the British Broadcasting Corporation – or the BBC, for short – in 1952.

> When David first started working in television, his boss thought his teeth were "too big" for him to be a presenter! He worked as a producer, camera operator, director and sound technician instead.

Still fascinated by nature and wildlife, David began to present programmes like *Animal Patterns*, teaching viewers about animal camouflage and behaviour. He preferred to film animals in their natural habitats, not in a TV studio. While presenting *Zoo Quest*, David travelled far and wide to find extraordinary creatures and describe them to his audience.

A WORLD IN COLOUR

Early television programmes were broadcast in black and white. But in 1965, David was put in charge of the TV channel BBC Two, just before it began to broadcast in colour. Now that viewers could see the whole rainbow, what should be shown? He chose a range of exciting shows, from art programmes to crazy comedies, that made the channel very popular.

But although David enjoyed running BBC Two, he missed presenting and making programmes himself, especially wildlife programmes. So in 1972, he left the BBC and returned to making TV. For a long time, he had wanted to film a huge series, tracking life on our planet from its earliest beginnings to the present day. In 1979, *Life on Earth* was broadcast for the first time – and it was revolutionary.

As he looked at fossils, jellyfish and sharks, David's excitement gave his viewers a sense of getting right up close to secretive and amazing creatures. New ways of filming were used to show tiny details of animal life; camera operators would wait for hours to see a particular creature, or create fake habitats so they could film while animals slept. Viewers could watch amazing experiences, like David and a gorilla meeting face to face. The next day, the gorilla and her children groomed David as though he was one of them!

Many more award-winning documentaries followed, examining all Earth's habitats and creatures. David and his crew constantly found new ways to film the natural world – in *The Trials of Life*, medical equipment used to look inside the human body allowed them to film inside an army ants' nest!

There are more than 20 species of plants and animals named after David, including a Caribbean bat (*Myotis attenboroughi*) and a Madagascan stump-toed frog (*Stumpffia davidattenboroughi*)!

David wasn't the only performer in the family. His brother Richard would go on to become an Oscar-winning actor and director, starring in films like *Jurassic Park*.

SAVING THE PLANET

David is especially well known for his two recent documentaries about ocean life – the beautiful and moving *Blue Planet* and *Blue Planet II*. One episode of *Blue Planet II*, which showed a whale grieving for her baby calf killed by plastic, made viewers aware of how badly plastic pollution affects marine life. It had a huge impact, encouraging many people to start using metal straws or canvas bags to avoid filling the sea with more plastic rubbish.

Though some of his earlier programmes were more gentle or hopeful about the environment, David Attenborough is now determined to tell everyone who watches his work that we must act now to save our world. All his life, he has shown the development of life on Earth, its astonishing riches and the ways in which human activity has harmed and threatened it. Now he is using all his experience to tell us to fight back against climate change and extinction.

SHIRLEY BASSEY

Born into poverty, with many struggles to overcome, Shirley Bassey would go on to become one of the world's most successful female singers, famous for singing James Bond themes – and for the sheer power of her voice!

SCRAPING BY

In the 1930s, life in the Tiger Bay docklands in Cardiff, Wales, could be tough. The docklands were full of sailors from all around the world, determined to enjoy themselves now they were back on dry land – sometimes in a very rowdy way. But Tiger Bay was also a place where people played all kinds of music, danced and had fun together.

In 1937, a baby girl was born there, the youngest of seven children, to Eliza, who had moved there from England, and Henry Bassey, a Nigerian seaman. Things were hard for the Bassey family. There were a lot of them and they didn't have much money. Back then, it was uncommon for white and Black people to marry, so they often faced racism and prejudice. The wider world was rumbling grimly towards the Second World War. And when Shirley was only one year old, her father was sent to prison, making it even harder for her mother to support Shirley and her sisters and brother. The family moved to another place, called Splott, not far away, and scraped by on Eliza's earnings.

ALWAYS SINGING

Shirley adored her mother, who was a good cook and very pretty – and who loved to dance. She didn't like the cheap meat the family had to eat, and being cold and wearing hand-me-down clothes, but she dreamed of better things – and she sang all the time, until her sisters told her to shut up!

When Shirley was a teenager, she left school and went to work in a factory to help pay the family's bills – though she got into trouble for singing on the job! At night, she also sang in pubs and clubs to earn some extra money. She had a lot of talent and appeared in a couple of touring shows.

As well as being good at singing, Shirley was a very sporty little girl – she was good at netball, baseball and cricket.

BECOMING A STAR

Then things changed for Shirley. An agent called Michael Sullivan heard her sing and her powerful voice impressed him so much that he offered to represent her, sure that he could make her a star. He taught Shirley how to stand and move on stage, so that she could keep an audience spellbound. Then she was invited to star in a show at the Adelphi Theatre, London. After she sang on TV and impressed a record company, she was offered a recording contract – and the chance to record her own songs.

When Shirley was 19, she released her first single, "Burn My Candle", and a year later she had her first big hit with "Banana Boat Song", which reached number eight in the charts. After that, there was no stopping her. In 1959, she became the first Welsh person to have a Number One hit with "As I Love You" – followed by a second Number One three years later.

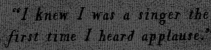

"I knew I was a singer the first time I heard applause."

INTERNATIONAL FAME

In 1964, Shirley sang her first James Bond theme song, "Goldfinger". This made her an international star, and was followed by two more – "Diamonds Are Forever" (1971) and "Moonraker" (1979). She began to go on tours around the world. Audiences were amazed by the power of her voice and the glamour of her presence. She became known for sequinned gowns, fabulous jewellery and sheer style!

GOLDFINGER
shirley bassey

Shirley played the Glastonbury Festival in 2007, stealing the show in a glamorous pink dress and diamanté Wellington boots. She also sang at Queen Elizabeth II's Diamond Jubilee. What did she sing? "Diamonds Are Forever", of course!

SHIRLEY BASSEY

Shirley went on to sell nearly 140 million records over the course of her career – and she is the only person ever to have recorded more than one James Bond theme. (She would still like to record another if she got the chance!) In 1999, she was made a Dame by Queen Elizabeth II, and in 2019, she was honoured by her hometown, Cardiff, and given an award called the 'Freedom of the City'.

MOONRAKER

ALEXANDER GRAHAM BELL

The brilliant Scotsman Alexander Graham Bell combined a lifelong interest in speech and communication with his love of science and inventing to give the world an amazing gift: the telephone.

INSPIRED TO LEARN

Alexander Bell was born in Edinburgh, Scotland, in 1847. (He chose to add Graham as his own middle name when he was 10!) He was the second son of Eliza Bell, who was deaf and used sign language, and Professor Alexander Melville Bell, a phonetician who studied how humans use sounds and other ways to talk to each other. He also taught elocution, which is the skill of speaking clearly. Because of his father's work, and his mother's deafness, Alexander was interested in speech and communication from very early on.

Until he was 11, Alexander was taught at home by his parents. Eliza was an especially inspiring teacher, encouraging him to work hard to reach his dreams – she was a talented musician herself, despite her hearing loss. After that, he was sent to school, but his marks were very bad! He was only interested in science, and often skipped lessons that he didn't like.

When Alexander was 15, he moved to London, where his grandfather, also an elocution teacher, made him feel ashamed of how little he knew. He inspired Alexander to learn more, especially about speech and how humans and animals make sounds to communicate.

Alexander went back to school in Scotland a year later. Here, he learned some Greek and Latin – and, like his father and grandfather, began to teach elocution himself. But he was still interested in science, and he liked to experiment and make his own inventions. At the age of 16, he and his brother Melville built a robot together.

Formal learning might not have suited Alexander, but his cleverness was clear. When he was 12, playing with a friend at a flour mill, he invented a machine to take the husks off the grains of wheat. This machine was used at the mill for several years!

SETTING UP SCHOOL

Sadly for the Bell family, both Alexander's brothers died of tuberculosis by the time he was 23. Alexander was such a hard worker that he often tired himself out, leaving him weak and at risk of illness. Desperately afraid that they would lose him too, Alexander's father moved the family to Canada, which he believed was a healthier place to live.

In 1871, Alexander moved to the USA and settled in Boston. Here, he opened a school devoted to helping deaf people learn to speak, building on his father's work. Alexander believed that deaf people should use speech rather than sign language so they could communicate with hearing people more easily – this made some deaf people angry, because he didn't recognise the value of different methods of communication.

While Alexander was living in Canada, he learned the language of the Mohawk people, and wrote it down – the first time the Mohawk language had been put on paper. For this, he was made an honorary chief.

AN INVENTIVE BRAIN

Alexander's interest in speech now mixed with his long-time love of inventing mechanical devices. He began to experiment and work towards transmitting the human voice over wires – making a 'vocal telegraph'. On 10th March 1876, after years of work and research with the skilled electrician Thomas Watson, Alexander made the first telephone call. The words he spoke were: "Mr Watson, come here – I want to see you."

In 1877, the Bell Telephone Company was set up. The same year, Alexander married one of his former students, Mabel Hubbard. Intelligent and business-like, Mabel managed their money – and even secretly booked Alexander's train ticket to make him go and demonstrate the telephone at a huge exhibition, which he didn't want to do. (He was grateful afterwards – the exhibition was a grand success!)

Alexander's inventive brain never stopped working. As well as the telephone, he later carried out research into flight, hydrofoils, metal detectors and even predicted global warming. He actually felt that his 'photophone' – a device which carried sounds on a beam of light – was his life's greatest invention.

By the time Alexander died, in 1922, he had travelled a long way from his Scottish birthplace, taught many deaf people – including the famous author Helen Keller – and helped to connect millions of people, across America and around the world. As a mark of respect, during his funeral, every telephone in North America was silenced.

"In scientific researches, there are no unsuccessful experiments; every experiment contains a lesson."

TIM BERNERS-LEE

The computer scientist Tim Berners-Lee invented the World Wide Web and was instrumental in the development of the Internet, which would completely change the way people communicate, buy things, work and learn forever.

FAMILY OF MATHEMATICIANS

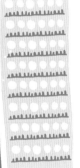

In the early 1950s, two mathematicians, Mary Lee Woods and Conway Berners-Lee, met and fell in love. They had a lot in common – in fact, they were both working on a computer called the Ferranti Mark 1, which was one of the first computers that people could buy!

In 1955, their first child was born in Richmond, London – a son called Timothy, who inherited his parents' mathematical gifts. As a little boy, Tim liked model railways and trainspotting. He was thoughtful and quiet and liked working things out. His parents encouraged him to use maths to solve problems, even at the dinner table! They also talked to him about computers and what these machines could 'understand' – and the potential they had to change people's lives.

PHYSICS AND TIDDLYWINKS

Tim's youngest brother, Mike, is an impressive scientist too – he's an expert on greenhouse gases!

Tim decided to study physics at Oxford University and was very good at it. He achieved a first-class degree, but he also got into trouble for hacking the university computer with a friend. As a punishment, he was banned from using it – so he built his own computer with a soldering iron and an old television! He also found the time to play tiddlywinks against Cambridge University.

PROGRAMMING GENIUS

After leaving university, Tim worked as a programmer for a company which made traffic lights. Then, for a while, he worked on software for CERN, the huge European physics laboratory. While he was there, Tim invented a program called ENQUIRE, which stored information in 'links' that allowed a user to move easily between files. This became known as 'hypertext'.

After that, Tim designed many different computer systems before he went back to CERN, this time to work on their computer network. In 1989, he made a plan to create a hypertext system that would join with the Internet – which connected computers around the world – to allow scientists to see each other's files and results without emailing all the time. It was this plan that would become the World Wide Web, uniting the scrappy beginnings of the Internet into a huge international network.

> *"The Web does not just connect machines, it connects people."*

THE WORLD WIDE WEB

When Tim was given permission to develop his idea, he went on to design and build the first web browser and editor. The first site on the World Wide Web went live on 6th August 1991. It explained what the Web was and how to set up a server.

Tim didn't realise then how important his invention would be, or how the Web's popularity would explode, changing the way people worked and learned and talked to each other. Without his work, we might have no Google, no Wikipedia, no YouTube – and the Internet might belong to just a few people with the special skills to use it or enough money to buy access to it. One of the most important things about the World Wide Web was that Tim made it available to everyone, without needing to pay or sign up to anything. He believes that the Web should remain open to all, and that everyone should be able to edit it and work within it. He also believes that scientists who work with computers have a duty to keep the Web a safe place for its users.

QUIET ACHIEVER

Tim has been honoured in many ways for his world-changing achievement. He is now Sir Tim Berners-Lee and holds positions at many universities. Time magazine named him one of the 100 Most Important People of the 20th century, and he was the first winner of Finland's Millennium Technology Prize. Despite his fame, Tim doesn't live like a celebrity. When he isn't writing code or meeting world leaders, he likes to spend time quietly with his family.

> *Tim was part of the London Olympics opening ceremony in 2012. As the invention of the World Wide Web was acted out, he tweeted: "This is for everyone".*

ANEURIN BEVAN

What do you know about the National Health Service? If you were born in Britain, you were probably born in a NHS hospital, with NHS midwives and doctors looking after you. When you have injections or visit a surgery if you're ill, that's usually part of the NHS too. Unlike in many other countries, you and your family don't have to pay to see a doctor. And this is thanks to Aneurin Bevan, the Welsh politician who set up the NHS after the end of the Second World War.

LIFE IN THE VALLEYS

Aneurin, often called Nye for short, was born in 1897 in Tredegar, a mining town in South Wales. His father was a miner and his mother was the daughter of a blacksmith. Together, they had 10 children (Nye was the sixth), but five of them didn't live long enough to grow up. There were strikes and unrest during his childhood, and poor people were often treated badly by the wealthy owners of mines and other businesses. Nye felt this injustice strongly.

Aneurin had a terrible stutter as a child, and his cruel headmaster hated him, but he was determined to overcome both these things. He educated himself by reading books from his local library and found that he could get the better of his stutter by shouting at the top of his voice! (He became well known later on for his booming speeches.) He also recited poetry he'd learned by heart on the hills above Tredegar.

At 13, Nye left school and started work in the mine with his father and brother, but he didn't stop learning – he carried on taking out books from the library and filling his mind with new knowledge. In 1925, his father died from lung disease – something that often killed miners, who had to breathe in coal dust and harmful gases as they worked. Nye had grown up surrounded by people whose harsh lives meant they were often ill. But in Tredegar, Nye had seen something else too. Many of the miners paid a small amount of their salary – 3 pence from every pound – into a fund so that they and their families could see a doctor when they needed to. In other places, if you couldn't pay, you often couldn't see a doctor at all and many people died because they couldn't afford treatment.

FOR THE PEOPLE

In 1919, Nye won a scholarship to study in London, where he decided that socialism – a system where a country's wealth is shared equally between its people – was a better way to run a country than capitalism, where people who own businesses have a lot of wealth and power. The rich factory and mine owners might not look after their workers or pay them fairly. Nye became a trade union activist, demanding better conditions for poor people.

Soon after this, Nye was chosen as a Member of Parliament (MP) for the Labour party, and became known for criticising other politicians whom he felt weren't on the side of working men and women. He got married to Jennie Lee, another Labour MP, in 1934. During the Second World War, which started in 1939, he often criticised the prime minister, Winston Churchill (page 34). This made him very unpopular, but he believed that many of Churchill's decisions were wrong.

Nye was proud to be a revolutionary. He described himself not as a politician but as "a projectile discharged from the Welsh valleys"!

BIRTH OF OUR

After the hardship of the war, many British people wanted a change. Churchill's Conservative party, which had been in charge of the country, was voted out and the Labour party came to power instead. Nye was given the job of Minister of Health. He was determined to make sure everyone in Britain could have medical treatment when they needed it, just as they had in Tredegar. Although many politicians were against it – as were a lot of doctors who wanted to carry on charging people for treatment! – the National Health Service Act was passed in 1946, and the NHS began treating people in 1948. This meant that thousands of people who couldn't afford to pay could now have medical care that improved or even saved their lives.

A LEGACY FOR ALL

In Parliament, Nye was known as a prickly, difficult figure, someone who would fight to defend the rights of the underdog – not always politely. When NHS charges for dental care and glasses were introduced in 1951, Nye resigned from his job in protest. But he remained someone who was loved and trusted by the people who had elected him.

When Nye died of stomach cancer at the age of 62, the whole nation mourned. MPs wept in Parliament, and one newspaper said that there was "sorrow at every street corner" in the South Wales valleys where he came from. But his legacy – free healthcare for everyone, whether they could pay for it or not – has looked after millions of people their whole lives long, from the cradle to the grave.

Nye was always on the side of the poor and the downtrodden. As he said himself: "I do not represent the big bosses at the top. I represent the people at the bottom."

MALORIE BLACKMAN

Malorie Blackman grew up reading and writing all the time – but she didn't dream that she would one day write books to inspire thousands of children and teenagers herself! Loved by readers of all ages, her books include the best-selling *Noughts and Crosses* series.

BARBADOS

LONDON

A NEW LONDON LIFE

Malorie Blackman's parents arrived in England in 1960 from Barbados in the Caribbean, hoping to make a new life for their family in Britain. Malorie was born in Surrey two years later, but she grew up mostly in Clapham, a part of London. When she was three, her mother had twin baby boys – Malorie loved helping to look after her brothers, though they were a lot of work! Not long after, her two older siblings, who had been living with relatives in Barbados, came to join them in England, and the whole family was complete.

Malorie loved books and reading as a child, especially myths and legends – one of her favourite books was *The Silver Chair* by C.S. Lewis, set in the magic land of Narnia, and filled with giants, strange underground creatures, a terrifying serpent, and a prince under a spell. She read it at least 10 times! By the age of 11, she'd read all the children's books in the library, a bit like Roald Dahl's Matilda (page 36). She also wrote stories and poems non-stop herself, but she didn't dream that she might become a published writer – partly because she was Black, and all the writers she knew of didn't look like she did.

Sometimes Malorie experienced racism directed towards her – like the ticket inspector who accused her of having stolen her first class ticket when she was a teenager, or the history teacher who told her that there had never been Black inventors, scientists or pioneers. They made her feel angry and sad – and determined to make a difference.

Stormzy (page 100) namechecks Malorie in his song "Superheroes"! The grime star has said how much he loved Noughts and Crosses when he was growing up – he even has a role in the TV adaptation.

NOT SO STUPID

Malorie had always wanted to become an English teacher, but she actually studied computing at college after the school careers adviser told her she shouldn't try to train as a teacher. She worked as a computer programmer for several years, but then she was drawn like a magnet back to the world of books and stories. She wrote her first book, *Not So Stupid!*, a collection of science fiction and horror stories for teenagers, when she was 28.

Though *Not So Stupid!* was turned down by publishers more than 80 times, it was eventually published in 1990. After that, there was no stopping Malorie! She went on to write more than 60 books, including *Pig Heart Boy*, about a boy who needs a heart transplant, *Hacker*, a mystery thriller, and *Cloud Busting*, a book told in different kinds of poetry. She also wrote stage plays and scripts for TV shows like *Byker Grove* and *Doctor Who*.

Malorie was the eighth Children's Laureate, between 2013 and 2015. As Laureate, she talked about how important it was for teenagers to read for pleasure, saying that they should read what they enjoy before being forced to dive into "the classics".

NOUGHTS AND CROSSES

In 2001, her most famous book, *Noughts and Crosses*, was published. Set in a world where Black people have been "history's lucky ones", rather than white people, it imagines what would happen in a world where Black people ('Crosses') are more powerful and rich than white ones ('Noughts'), and if a Nought boy and a Cross girl were to fall in love. Malorie wrote six more books in the series – and *Noughts and Crosses* is now one of the most-read books for teenagers in the country. Malorie's books for all ages, from toddlers to teens, have inspired and delighted countless readers – and proved to many kids that brilliant writers are not just white.

Malorie has lots of hobbies. She plays the piano, drums, learns languages, composes music and loves to play World of Warcraft.

WILLIAM BLAKE

Although he was often thought to be mad during his lifetime, William Blake is now considered one of Britain's most talented poets and artists. His vivid creations, full of monsters and angels, fairies and devils, look like no other artist's work.

UNUSUAL LITTLE BOY

In 1757, Britain and France were at war, squabbling over colonies in different parts of the world. Rumblings of revolution were starting up around the globe, and new ideas of fairness, science and human rights were starting to take over from old traditions of respecting the rich and powerful.

At home in London, in the poor area of Soho, a little boy was born to a couple called James and Catherine Blake. His father was a 'hosier', a person who sold stockings, and his mother looked after William and his five siblings, and educated them mostly at home. They didn't have a lot of money and Soho wasn't a very healthy place to live – two of William's brothers died when they were babies. But they were thoughtful, caring parents, especially when it came to their unusual son.

William was quite a strange little boy. From early on, he sometimes saw things that others didn't – when he was four, he saw a vision of God at the window, which scared him so much that he screamed! When he was nine, he passed a tree in a park that seemed to him to be covered in angels.

His parents were Dissenters, meaning they were Christians but disagreed with the teachings of the Church of England. This meant William grew up with a strong belief in God, but with his own way of being a Christian, which would later be very important to his work. He read the Bible all the time, loving its stories and poetry.

MAKING PICTURES

Young William loved making pictures too. Rather than drawing, he preferred engraving – using a sharp tool to make lines on a metal plate. He engraved pictures of ancient Greek statues and objects, and his parents gave him lots of books and pictures to copy, which was all they could afford.

The Blakes understood that William – who knew his own mind and went his own way – wouldn't do well at a strict school. They continued to teach him at home, although he also studied at a drawing school until he became an apprentice to an engraver called James Basire at age 14. He worked with Basire for seven years, and then became an engraver himself. Because he wanted to be a painter, he also studied at the Royal Academy of Art.

POETRY AND PAINTING

William believed strongly in women's rights. He felt that no one should have to marry someone they didn't love.

In 1782, William married a woman called Catherine Boucher. Catherine couldn't read or write, but William taught her to do both, as well as how to engrave. He ran a print shop for a while, but he mostly earned his living by illustrating other people's books. In 1783, he published his first collection of poetry.

As well as engraving, William painted watercolour pictures. He painted things like scenes from the Bible, ghosts, angels and devils. When his brother Robert died in 1787, he had a vision of Robert's spirit rising to heaven, clapping its hands. This had a powerful effect on his later work.

In 1789, William printed, bound and published a book called *Songs of Innocence*, followed five years later by *Songs of Experience*. *Songs of Innocence* was about the innocence of children, while *Songs of Experience* dealt with the harshness of adulthood. William illustrated both of them with engravings coloured to look like medieval manuscripts, using a special method of combining text and pictures that he had invented himself.

William published other works of poetry too, full of religion and his own made-up mythology, but *Songs of Innocence* and *Songs of Experience* are now his best-known works. Most people considered his paintings and poetry strange, impossible to understand – but some bought them anyway, finding them fascinating as well as weird.

One of William's most famous poems was called "The Tyger". Its first verse goes like this: "Tyger Tyger, burning bright, In the forests of the night, What immortal hand or eye Could frame thy fearful symmetry?"

UNRECOGNISED IN HIS OWN LIFETIME

In 1800, William moved to a place called Felpham to start a new job. Here, he got into a fight with a soldier called John Schofield, who accused William of insulting the king. In those days, this was a serious crime! William was taken to court, but luckily he was found not guilty. In 1803, he and Catherine moved back to London, the place that had always inspired William most.

Because his work was so unique, William was often thought to be mad – he certainly wasn't considered a brilliant artist in his lifetime. When he held an exhibition above his brother's shop in 1809, very few people came. The one critic who did write about it called his work "the wild effusions of a distempered brain"! William died in 1827, and was buried in Bunhill Fields in London. He is now considered one of the greatest British artists and poets of all time.

BOUDICCA

We don't know much about the life of the warrior queen Boudicca (also spelled Boudica and Boadicea), because she lived so long ago. Everything we do know comes from two Roman historians, Tacitus and Cassius Dio, but they wrote a lot about the woman who caused the Romans so much trouble! They showed Boudicca as a strong, fascinating figure, a commander who could lead a group of wild tribes against the powerful armies of the Roman Empire – and win.

BORN WARRIOR

In around CE 30, a baby girl was born near the town of Camulodunum (now Colchester in Essex), probably to a royal family who ruled a local group of people called a 'tribe'. Her name was Boudicca, from a Celtic word *boud,* meaning 'victory' – a powerful name for the warrior she would become. As she grew up, she was trained to use weapons like swords, spears and javelins, just like the other girls in her tribe.

When she was about 18 years old, Boudicca married Prasutagas, king of the Iceni tribe, who lived in what's now Norfolk, East Anglia. Although the Romans had taken over the Iceni lands, they had agreed that Prasutagas could still be king of the tribe. The Iceni did have to pay high taxes, and they were sometimes treated badly, but they were at peace with the Romans – for now.

All that changed, though, when Prasutagas died in CE 60. He left a will in which he gave all his wealth to his daughters and to the Roman emperor Nero. But Romans did not allow girls or women to inherit, so the Empire decided to take the lot. Soldiers stole all the Iceni's land and goods, Boudicca was publicly beaten, and her two young daughters were badly injured. Hurt and furious, Boudicca rose in revolt.

Cassius Dio said that Boudicca *"was very tall, terrifying in appearance, with a most fierce glance and a harsh voice". She had "a great mass of the fieriest hair down to her hips",* and wore a thick gold neck ring called a 'torc', and a striped tunic under a cloak fastened with a brooch – definitely someone you would remember meeting!

THE UPRISING

The Romans had also angered other tribes nearby, so Boudicca joined forces with them. With her daughters by her side, Boudicca got into her chariot and rode on Camulodunum, which was now an important stronghold for the Romans. Retired soldiers had been seizing homes and food from the Britons who lived there, so many people were ready to rebel. The town wasn't well defended, and the Roman governor Suetonius was away, fighting in Wales.

In just a few days, Boudicca and her allies sacked the city, cut the head off the statue of Nero there, demolished its buildings and killed its inhabitants. They went on to destroy almost the entire Ninth Legion: several thousand skilled Roman soldiers.

Next, Boudicca and her armies marched on Londinium (London) and Verulamium (St Albans), where they continued to crush their enemies. Suetonius had rushed back from Wales. Realising he did not have enough troops to defend Londinium, he pulled back, and allowed Boudicca's forces to burn it to the ground. In total, 70,000–80,000 Romans had been killed since Boudicca started fighting.

However, Suetonius had now managed to gather 10,000 troops together. He stationed them in a narrow gorge backed by a forest, to protect his forces from attack on three sides. Although he was heavily outnumbered, he arranged his soldiers with care, while the Britons (according to Tacitus) were careless, even bringing their families in carts to watch the battle.

Before the fight began, Boudicca drove her war-chariot through the ranks and spoke to encourage her troops, reminding them of the pain and injustice they had suffered at Roman hands. But this last battle was to be the end, both of Boudicca's victories and of her life. Suetonius's soldiers marched in a tight 'wedge' formation and sent showers of arrows into the group of Britons, who were chaotic and disorganised. As they fled, falling over the carts they'd brought to the battlefield, the Romans killed them in huge numbers. Boudicca, seeing that they had lost the fight, either poisoned herself or died of shock.

> *According to Tacitus, Boudicca said this in her last speech: "Britons have been led to battle by women before. But I have not come to boast of my noble ancestors, or even to get back my kingdom and my family's stolen wealth. I am fighting, like any of you, for freedom, and to take revenge for my beaten body and my shamefully injured daughters . . . We must conquer or die here. This I have decided, as a woman – you men may choose to live as slaves."*

ICON OF REBELLION

Though her revolt against the Romans ultimately failed, Boudicca came close to driving them out of Britannia. She is now a powerful symbol of rebellion, especially for feminists. A statue of Boudicca, triumphant in a chariot and brandishing a spear, stands near the Houses of Parliament in London.

CHARLOTTE BRONTË

One of three talented Brontë sisters who grew up to write brilliant books, Charlotte told stories of powerless women and girls – and the passion and fire they had to keep locked up inside them.

A YEAR WITHOUT A SUMMER

In 1816, a cold, wet year that would later be called "a year without a summer", a baby girl called Charlotte was born in the Yorkshire village of Thornton. The third daughter of an Irish vicar called Patrick Brontë and his wife Maria, she grew up in another village called Haworth. She lived with her parents, four sisters and her brother, Branwell, in a big house that backed onto the moors. Her mother died when she was five – but Maria, her eldest sister, behaved like a mother to Charlotte and the others, reading to them from newspapers and looking after them as tenderly as she could.

However, in 1824, Charlotte and all her sisters except Anne, the youngest, were sent away to the Clergy Daughters' School in a place called Cowan Bridge, Lancashire. This school was a miserable place. The children wore plain, uncomfortable uniforms, received very little to eat, had to wash in freezing water and were harshly punished for mistakes or untidiness. There was also an outbreak of an illness called typhus while the Brontë sisters were there. Weakened by their bad living conditions, Charlotte's two elder sisters, Maria and Elizabeth, died from the illness. Charlotte never forgave the clergyman who ran the school. She later wrote about it in her book *Jane Eyre*.

When Charlotte and Emily came home from school, they wrote and invented stories non-stop. All four remaining Brontë children made up imaginary worlds, with names like Gondal, Angria and Glasstown. They wrote stories and poems about the wars and plots and murders that happened there. They also ran wild, playing on the windy moors that stretched out behind their house. In 1831, Charlotte went away again to a different school, but she left a year later, and came home to teach her sisters what she had learned.

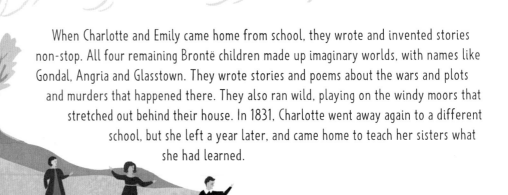

CURRER BELL

As adults, Charlotte and Emily left home to earn a living as governesses, teaching the children of well-off families. Governesses weren't treated very well – they weren't servants, but they weren't members of the family either. They were paid badly, and as soon as their pupils grew too old to need them, they lost their jobs! In her books, Charlotte wrote about being a governess too.

Charlotte published *Jane Eyre* in 1847, when she was 31 – but she had to publish it using a man's name, Currer Bell. Women weren't usually expected to write books at that time and women's writing wasn't thought to be any good! *Jane Eyre* was the story of an orphan girl, poor and plain but passionate and rebellious, who falls in love with her rich employer, only to discover that he has a terrible secret. It was a huge success.

Emily and Anne also became successful and famous writers, publishing under the names *Ellis* and *Acton Bell*. Emily's famous novel *Wuthering Heights* was a story of doomed love and cruelty, while Anne's *The Tenant of Wildfell Hall* was considered scandalous at the time. It portrayed a woman leaving her husband, and making a new life for herself and her son.

A POWERFUL VOICE

Although *Jane Eyre* was her best-known book, Charlotte published two other novels as well. But her own life was filled with tragedy – Branwell died in 1848, soon followed by Emily and Anne, leaving the house in Haworth almost empty. Charlotte continued to write, but she missed her sisters.

She had several proposals of marriage, but she turned them all down until she married Arthur Bell Nicholls in 1854, a priest who worked with her father. Sadly, she didn't get the chance to enjoy a long life of happiness with him – the next year, pregnant and very sick, she died at the early age of 39. But the passion of her voice, demanding respect and freedom for powerless women and children, would ring out strong for years and years to come.

ROBERT THE BRUCE

Robert the Bruce, who became King of Scots in 1306, was a powerful ruler and fighter who won Scotland independence from England in the Middle Ages, and is still considered a Scottish national hero.

SON OF A NOBLE FAMILY

Born in 1274 at Turnberry Castle in Ayrshire, Robert was the third of 10 children, and the eldest of his parents' sons. His ancestor David I had been king of Scotland, and his father was a land-owning lord. His mother, Marjorie, was Countess of Carrick, a powerful woman in her own right. There's a legend that she held Robert's father – also called Robert – captive and said she would only release him if he promised to marry her!

We don't know a lot about Robert's childhood because it was so long ago. As the son of a noble family, he would have grown up speaking Anglo-Norman French as well as Scottish Gaelic, and learned Latin, which was the language of law and religion. He would also have been trained to ride, use a sword, joust with a lance, and hunt. He loved reading when he was older, especially the histories of other kings, in which he saw echoes of his own life. As the oldest son, he knew he would inherit his father's title, so he probably felt responsible for the family lands and the people who lived there too.

In 1290, when Robert was 16, the queen of Scotland died, and the empty throne was claimed by 13 different noblemen, including Robert's grandfather. To avoid war between the noblemen, Edward I, the king of England, was asked to choose who should rule Scotland next. After two years, Edward appointed a man called John Balliol to the Scottish throne. The Bruce family were very disappointed.

When John Balliol argued with Edward and went to war with him, the Bruces supported the English king against their old rival. Balliol was forced to give up the throne in 1296. The Bruces hoped, once again, that Robert's grandfather would take over as king. Instead, Edward began to rule Scotland as a part of England.

KING OF SCOTS

Then a group of Scottish noblemen, led by John Comyn, Balliol's nephew, turned against the Bruces and drove them out of Scotland. The Bruces went to live in Carlisle Castle in England, given to them by Edward I. When Comyn's army attacked Carlisle, Edward drove them back – and the Bruces fought with him on the English side. However, in 1297, Robert decided to join the rebels who were fighting against Edward for Scottish independence.

At the Battle of Falkirk in 1298, Edward defeated the rebels, but he forgave Robert and didn't take away his lands. Instead, Robert and his old enemy John Comyn became joint Guardians of Scotland – but they didn't get on with each other any better. In 1306, Robert got into a quarrel with John Comyn and killed him. Edward was furious and Robert began making plans with the rebels to take over the kingdom. Scotland was plunged into civil war, as well as war with England.

Robert was quickly crowned King of Scots, but he had to stay in hiding for a long time. Many Scottish people were still angry with him because he had murdered Comyn.

There is a story that after his disastrous first year as king, Robert was hiding in a cave and saw a spider try again and again to spin a web, until it succeeded. This inspired him to continue his fight against the English.

AN INDEPENDENT SCOTLAND

Robert began to carry out raids on the towns and cities that were loyal to Comyn, and slowly win them over to his side. He was lucky – Edward I, who was a great military leader, died in 1307 before he could crush Robert's rebellion. His son, Edward II, was more timid. He agreed to a truce, which gave Robert time to settle in. In 1309, Robert set up his own parliament at St Andrews in the east of Scotland. When he started capturing castles from the English, Edward II realised he would have to act. In 1314, he took an army to challenge Robert at Bannockburn, near Stirling.

At Bannockburn, although they were outnumbered, Robert's forces won the battle against Edward II. This didn't drive the English out of Scotland altogether, but it united the Scottish people in support of Robert.

In 1328, Robert and Edward III of England signed the Treaty of Edinburgh–Northampton, which declared Scotland to be an independent country, ruled by Robert as its king. Robert had at last achieved what he'd set out to do – have Scotland's independence recognised by England and the wider world. He died the following year, and his son became the new king.

Scotland would remain a separate kingdom until 1603, when Scotland and England were once again ruled by the same king, James VI of Scotland (also known as James I of England). This led to the union of the two countries again.

Robert was extremely ambitious, and could be sneaky, switching sides when it suited him. He also showed no mercy to his enemies. But he was a brave and clever fighter, and the wise laws he made won him the name Good King Robert.

ISAMBARD KINGDOM BRUNEL

The brilliant engineer and inventor Isambard Kingdom Brunel was born in 1806, in the busy coastal city of Portsmouth. By the time he died, 53 years later, his bridges, tunnels, ships and railways had revolutionised travel, broken speed limits and exploded ideas about the uses of iron and stone. He has been called "the father of the Industrial Revolution", as well as "the man who built Britain".

THE BRUNEL FAMILY

Isambard inherited his gift for inventing from his father, Marc, a French engineer who had fled his home country during the French Revolution. When Marc Brunel came to Britain in 1799, the Navy asked him to set up a new system of machines for making special parts for ships on the Portsmouth docks. This was the world's first mass production line. Now safe in Portsmouth, Marc Brunel married his English fiancée, Sophia Kingdom, and they had three children: Sophia, Emma and Isambard.

Even as a little boy, Isambard was attracted to engineering and inventing. Marc was delighted – his own father had been very angry when Marc became an engineer. Determined that his son should get the best possible education, he taught six-year-old Isambard scale drawing and geometry, and, although it was expensive, sent him away to boarding school when he was eight. After that, Isambard went to school in France and then went to work as an apprentice for a brilliant watchmaker called Breguet, who spotted that he had a gift for invention.

After Isambard finished studying in 1822, he returned to Britain to work with his father. When Marc began an ambitious project to build a tunnel under the Thames, Isambard joined his father as assistant engineer. Everything went well until 1828, when the tunnel flooded, killing six workers and almost drowning Isambard, who was badly injured. It took him months to recover.

While he was getting better, he heard of a competition to build a bridge over the deep, wide Avon Gorge in Clifton, Bristol – a bridge that (at the time) would be the longest in the world.

If you've ever been to Paddington Station in London, you've been inside one of Isambard's amazing designs. There's a statue of him between platforms 8 and 9, holding his trademark tall 'stovepipe' hat – though Isambard himself was only 1.52 metres tall!

BRIDGES AND RAILWAYS

Isambard couldn't resist the challenge. He instantly threw himself into designing a magnificent suspension bridge, where the roadway hangs from cables held up by towers. He eventually won the competition, even though his rival, the engineer Thomas Telford, told the judges to use his designs instead. Work began on the bridge, but sadly the money ran out before it could be finished. It wasn't completed until after Isambard's death – although it would later be considered one of his greatest achievements.

After that, Isambard turned his attention to the railways, a new invention that was just beginning to challenge other ways of travel by road or canal. When he was only 27, he was made Chief Engineer of the Great Western Railway, which was an important line being built to connect London and the south-west of England. Ever ambitious, Isambard wanted his railway line to be the longest, smoothest and broadest in Britain.

He decided that a 'wide gauge' track, almost double the width of other lines, would allow trains to be more stable – and to travel faster. He also built viaducts, stations and tunnels on the line in his drive to improve it, including the two-mile-long Box Tunnel, which took six years to complete!

> *While working on the bridge, the daring Isambard once travelled across the gorge in a basket dangling from an iron bar!*

TAKING TO THE SEA

From the Great Western Railway to the Great Steamship Company, Isambard next looked at the idea of travel by sea. Before now, only sailing ships, which used the power of the wind to travel, had crossed the Atlantic Ocean. People believed that steamships, powered by burning coal, just couldn't carry enough fuel for the whole voyage. Isambard had never made a ship before, but he didn't let that stop him! He designed and built a steamship called the *SS Great Western*, the biggest and longest ever made. Although he was badly burned in a fire on board, he carried on – and his huge ship made the trans-Atlantic crossing in just 13 days, with plenty of coal left over. His next vessel was the *SS Great Britain*, one of the very first propeller-driven ships, and the first to be built from iron, rather than wood. His last was the *SS Great Eastern*, a double-hulled giant intended to carry 4,000 passengers all the way to Australia.

Isambard had worked furiously hard all his life, although he had found time to get married to Mary Horsley in 1836, and to have three children (one of whom, his son Henry, would also grow up to be an engineer.) Sadly, his brilliant, inventive work was cut short – he died of a stroke in 1859, aged only 53, before the *SS Great Eastern* made her first voyage. In his lifetime, Isambard was often thought too wild to be taken seriously, but his achievements are now legendary – a refugee's son who changed the landscape of Britain forever.

> *As well as ships, bridges, tunnels and railways, Isambard once designed a hospital! During the Crimean War, injured British soldiers caught a lot of diseases because they were treated in dirty places. Isambard designed a hygienic hospital made of wood, with parts that could be sent to the battlefields and built there.*

EDITH CAVELL

Brave, compassionate and determined, Edith Cavell was a skilled nurse who trained many others, improved nursing standards, and eventually gave her life during the First World War helping wounded soldiers get to safety.

A VILLAGE CHILDHOOD

In the winter of 1865, a little girl called Edith Cavell was born in a village in Norfolk. Her father was the vicar there, and she lived for most of her childhood in a smart house with her parents and three younger siblings, Florence, Lilian and John. Although their house was grand, the family didn't have a lot of money – it had all been spent on building the house! Whenever they had a hot meal, they shared it with poorer people in the village, and Edith learned early on how hard life could be for people with very little.

As the daughter of a vicar, Sundays could seem boring. The children had to go to Sunday school as well as church, and they weren't allowed to read books (except the Bible) or play cards. Edith found her father's sermons especially dull! Frederick Cavell was a strict father, but also a kind one – if his children asked him to, he would often chase them through the house, roaring like a bear. Young Edith enjoyed painting, especially flowers, and became so good at it that she sometimes painted boxes as gifts for people in the village. She also loved ice-skating on the frozen moat behind the church. The first school she went to was four and a half miles from her home – she walked all the way there and back, every day.

When she was a teenager, Edith went to three different boarding schools. At the last one, Laurel Court, she learned to speak French very well, and was trained to become a teacher herself. When she left school, she went to work as a governess for a family in Essex, taking care of four children. Like her father, she knew how to be both kind and strict, and her pupils got on well with her. She loved tennis and dancing too – she once danced all night and ruined her shoes! In 1890, at the age of 25, Edith moved to Brussels to work for another family with four children, where she became fluent in French.

NOT AFRAID OF DANGER

When Edith was 30 years old, a big change happened in her life. Her father became ill, and she went home to nurse him. This made her decide that she wanted to train as a nurse – and so, when he had recovered, she started her training at the Royal London Hospital.

Edith was a very good nurse and she wasn't afraid of putting herself in danger. In 1897, when an attack of a disease called typhoid broke out in Kent, Edith went to help look after people who had caught it. She was given a medal for her work there – and she hadn't even finished her training yet! After this, she continued to work as a nurse for several years, often taking care of poor people, and running nursing homes as the matron in charge. She was so good at her job that a well-known doctor asked her to come and run a training programme for nurses in Belgium too.

Edith's training programme was so well thought of that Queen Elisabeth of Belgium asked for one of Edith's nurses when she broke her arm!

FAITHFUL UNTIL DEATH

In 1914, the First World War broke out. Edith stayed in Belgium, even after it was occupied by the invading German forces – she was determined to treat all injured soldiers in her clinic, whichever country they came from. Edith was not supposed to have anything to do with the war – the Germans would only allow her to continue working if she didn't get involved with the British or French forces, who they were fighting. However, feeling that it was her duty as a nurse, she began sheltering wounded British and French soldiers and helping them to cross the border into the Netherlands, which was not involved in the war. After several months, during which she helped over 150 men to leave occupied Belgium, she was betrayed and arrested. She was questioned for several days, accused of 'war treason' and condemned to die. Although foreign officials tried to stop it, she was executed by firing squad on 12th October 1915. She was only 49 years old.

After she died, people in many countries, particularly Britain, were told her story. Today, Edith Cavell is remembered as a nurse who saved the lives of soldiers on both sides without prejudice, and who gave her own life to help bring others to safety. A statue of her stands near Trafalgar Square, inscribed with the words 'Humanity' and 'Faithful until death'.

On the night before her execution, Edith Cavell told the priest who had been allowed to see her of her beliefs: "Patriotism is not enough. I must have no hatred or bitterness for anyone."

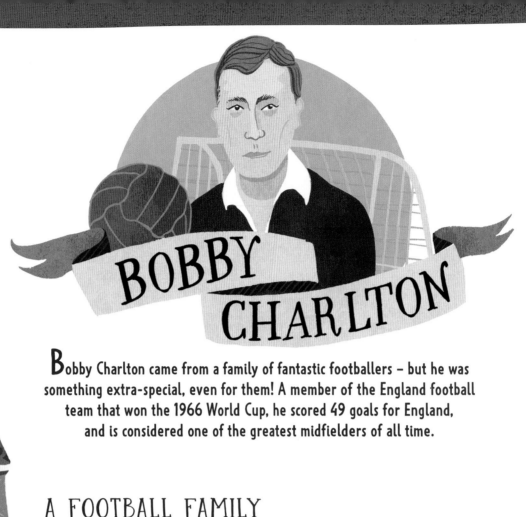

BOBBY CHARLTON

Bobby Charlton came from a family of fantastic footballers – but he was something extra-special, even for them! A member of the England football team that won the 1966 World Cup, he scored 49 goals for England, and is considered one of the greatest midfielders of all time.

A FOOTBALL FAMILY

On 11th October 1937, in the coal-mining town of Ashington, Northumberland, a woman called Elizabeth gave birth to a baby boy called Robert, named after his dad, Robert Charlton. Elizabeth (whom most people called Cissie) was known for her sparkling eyes and her mischievous sense of humour. Though she worked as a teacher, she loved football passionately and knew a lot about it. Her four brothers also loved football – in fact, they all played professionally. Jackie Milburn, her cousin, was a famous striker with Newcastle United too.

Cissie had wanted to be a football player herself, but back then, girls weren't able to become professional football players. Instead, she encouraged young Bobby and his brother Jack to play football, even though their dad was much more interested in boxing!

From an early age, it was clear that both boys were very talented, especially Bobby. But nobody knew that this little boy would grow up to become one of the greatest footballers ever to play for England.

Jack was outgoing and mischievous, but Bobby was so quiet and well behaved that he was nicknamed 'Little Lord Fauntleroy'!

MANCHESTER UNITED

Bobby joined Manchester United when he was only 15, still a schoolboy. Even though Cissie was so keen on football, she worried that Bobby wouldn't be able to earn a living playing 'the beautiful game' – so Bobby started an apprenticeship in electrical engineering too, just in case. But he soon signed professionally with Manchester United and never looked back.

At that time, United didn't have the amazing reputation they have now. They weren't a very successful team until manager Matt Busby hired and trained the set of incredibly talented players who would become known as the 'Busby Babes'. Bobby was one of the 'Babes', working his way up through the youth and reserve teams. He got his chance to play on the first team in 1956, scoring twice against Charlton Athletic – with a sprained ankle!

But in February 1958, a terrible tragedy happened. A plane carrying the Manchester United team, including Bobby, crashed on the runway at Munich-Riem Airport, Germany. Eight players were killed.

Bobby survived, but the club struggled after the disaster, and several of the survivors never played football again.

It was hard for Bobby to recover from the accident and the sad loss of his teammates. However, a few weeks later, he managed to get back out on the pitch again – and in April 1958 he played in the England squad for the first time, scoring against Scotland.

Over his career, Bobby Charlton scored an incredible **249** goals for Manchester United, and **49** goals for the English national team – only Wayne Rooney has scored more!

FOOTBALLER OF THE YEAR

Bobby would go on to play for England over 100 times during the course of his career. However, some of his most famous games happened during the 1966 World Cup. He scored both winning goals in England's semi-final against Portugal. And although he didn't score in the final against West Germany – which England won 4–2 – he was voted European Footballer of the Year for his brilliant playing throughout the tournament.

In 1973, aged 36, Bobby left Manchester United after 20 hugely successful years playing for the club. He became the manager of Preston North End for a while, and later returned to United to help run the club as a director.

Bobby won many awards and trophies during his career. In 1994 he was made a knight, becoming Sir Bobby Charlton, and in 2008 he was given the BBC Sports Personality of the Year Lifetime Achievement Award – which was presented to him by his brother Jack.

As a young man, Bobby's brother Jack worked as a miner and applied to become a police officer – but the lure of football was too strong for him, and he ended up playing for Leeds United! He also played with Bobby in the England team which won the 1966 World Cup, and eventually went on to become a brilliant manager for the Republic of Ireland team. He died in 2020.

WINSTON CHURCHILL

As prime minister, Winston Churchill led Britain through the Second World War, inspiring people with his speeches and refusing to give up, however terrible things seemed.

A POWERFUL FAMILY

Winston Spencer Churchill was born in 1874 to a very powerful family. His father was a British lord and a Member of Parliament (MP) and his mother was the daughter of a wealthy American businessman. He was born in a grand house called Blenheim Palace that had belonged to his father's family for generations.

Despite his family's power and wealth, Winston's childhood wasn't especially happy. He didn't see very much of his parents, although he thought his mother was beautiful and glamorous, "like the evening star". Like most upper-class Victorian boys, he was sent away to a boarding school when he was only seven. Here, children were taught Latin and Greek, and punished harshly if they didn't do well. Winston did not enjoy learning Latin and did not get very good marks in his lessons. When he was older, he took the entrance exam for a very well known boarding school called Harrow. He only just managed to pass the exam to be allowed to go there! Although he liked this school better – he learned to become a brilliant public speaker there, despite having a stutter and a lisp – he looked back on his school days as "a sombre grey patch upon the chart of my journey".

After seeing Winston playing with his huge collection of toy soldiers, his father was determined that he should join the army. It took him three tries to get into Sandhurst, a military academy that trained officers for the British Army. However, he eventually managed it. In 1895, when he had finished his training, he joined the Royal Cavalry (a group of soldiers who ride on horseback).

Winston was known for his courage on the battlefield, and he always wanted to be where the action was. During his time in the army, he served in India and Sudan. In 1899, at the start of the Boer War – a conflict between the British Empire and two independent states in South Africa – he travelled out to the battlefield as a journalist, reporting on the war. Then, like his father, he became an MP – and he was soon well known as a powerful speaker. However, during the First World War, he was in charge of a disastrous attack on Turkey, which went so badly, with so many people dying, that he was forced to resign. Winston thought his political career was over.

> *"In casting up this dread balance sheet . . . I see great reason for intense vigilance and exertion, but none whatever for panic or despair."*

SPEECHES THAT INSPIRED THE NATION

But 20 years later, just as the Second World War with Germany broke out, Winston became incredibly important to Britain. Before fighting began, he had warned the prime minister, Neville Chamberlain, that Adolf Hitler, the leader of the Nazi Party which ruled Germany, was dangerous.

After Neville Chamberlain resigned in 1940, shortly after the start of the war, Winston became prime minister. He worked closely with the American and Russian leaders to fight the Nazis. He refused to consider surrendering, even when the situation seemed desperate, and he gave speech after speech that inspired and united Britain to keep on fighting.

During the Battle of Britain, when German aircraft attacked Britain for months, trying to force Winston and the government to give up, the Royal Air Force fought them back again and again. Winston paid tribute to the courage of the British pilots: "Never in the field of human conflict was so much owed by so many to so few."

The determination shown by Winston and the British people paid off. Britain wasn't invaded. In 1945, Germany surrendered, and the Second World War was over.

> *Throughout his life, Winston was affected by depression, which he called "my black dog".*

HERO OF THE TIME

Although Winston was voted out of power at the end of the war, he became prime minister again between 1951 and 1955, and he remained very popular. When he died, in 1965, at the age of 90, he was given a state funeral – an honour usually only given to members of the royal family.

While Winston is generally considered a hero for what he did during the Second World War, he also held some very racist views. He said that African and Indian people were inferior to white people, a belief some people criticised at the time. In 1943, when Britain still controlled India, there was a terrible famine in the Bengal region of India and up to 3 million people died. Some historians say Winston didn't do enough to help the people living there, and that his decisions actually made things worse. Although he was a remarkable and talented man, who led Britain successfully through a time of war, his inspiring actions do not mean we can't recognise his faults – and expect better today.

> *Winston loved animals, especially cats, pigs and dogs. During the Second World War, his poodle Rufus sneaked into a government meeting. Winston told him he hadn't asked him to join the wartime cabinet!*

ROALD DAHL

Have you ever dreamed of eating a Wonka Bar, moving things with your mind, or making a potion that sent your grandma through the roof? Roald Dahl's amazing stories have been thrilling children – and grown-ups! – since *James and the Giant Peach* was published in 1961.

PRANKS AND CHOCOLATE

Roald Dahl was born in Llandaff, South Wales, in 1916, but his parents, Sofie and Harald, were Norwegian. Named after the famous polar explorer Roald Amundsen, Roald would also grow up to travel far and wide, especially in his imagination. In the summer holidays, he loved visiting his grandparents in Norway, where he ate fish pudding and special many-layered cake, and listened to his mother telling stories of trolls, giants and witches.

But Roald's childhood was marked by sadness, as well as joy and adventure. When he was only four, his sister Astri died of appendicitis, and not long after, his father died too. His mother was left with six children to bring up alone.

Roald was quite a mischievous little boy. He wrote about his experiences at school in Llandaff, and later at boarding school in Repton, in his autobiography, *Boy*. One of his most outrageous pranks was when he and a group of friends put a dead mouse in a bottle of gobstoppers! When the owner of the sweet shop complained, the headmaster punished the boys so harshly that Sofie took Roald away and sent him to another school. At boarding school in Repton, Roald hated the teachers' cruelty and having to run errands for older boys – but he loved being asked to test new chocolates for Cadbury and write down what he thought of them. This would inspire one of his most famous and best-loved books: *Charlie and the Chocolate Factory*.

FLYING THE NEST

When he left school, Roald didn't want to go to university – he wanted to find a job that would send him to some of the world's most beautiful and far-flung places. He joined the Shell Petroleum Company and went to Tanzania in East Africa.

When the Second World War broke out, in 1939, Roald joined the Royal Air Force and was taught to fly a fighter plane. Cramming himself into the tiny cockpit was very uncomfortable for him, as he was almost 2 metres tall! Roald was a gifted pilot, but one day his plane crash-landed in Egypt and he was seriously injured. He spent the rest of the war working at a desk.

Before Roald Dahl's stories, hardly anyone knew the word 'gremlin' – meaning a little mischievous creature that makes machinery go wrong. He learned it working in the RAF, and used it for his book, *The Gremlins*, published in 1943. Roald also invented more than 500 new words and names during his writing career!

WRITING STORIES

After the war Roald began making his living as a writer, mainly writing stories for grown-ups. In 1953, he married a film actor, Patricia Neal, and they had five children together. Through telling his children bedtime stories, Roald learned how to hold their attention and make them laugh – and he started to put these skills to use when writing his first children's books.

When *James and the Giant Peach* – the story of a little boy with two cruel aunts, a huge peach and some enormous insects – was published in 1961, it was an instant hit. After that, Roald went on to write over 20 books for children, including *Charlie and the Chocolate Factory*, *Fantastic Mr Fox*, *George's Marvellous Medicine*, *Matilda*, *The Twits*, *The Witches*, *Danny, the Champion of the World* and *The BFG*. The story of Matilda – a little girl with horrible parents, who loves reading and uses the power of her mind to move objects and fight back against cruel grown-ups – is one of Roald's best-known and best-loved tales.

Gruesome or scary things often happen in Roald's books – children may be eaten by giants, turned into mice, sucked up pipes or shrunk to a tiny size – but his tough, clever young heroes still come out on top, and young readers still love his stories! His books have sold more than 200 million copies worldwide.

Roald wasn't perfect though – he could be outspoken, and he held some prejudiced views about Jewish people that were hurtful and wrong. In 2020, his family apologised for the harm these views caused.

Roald died in 1990, when he was 74 years old, leaving behind a legacy of wonderful words and strange, exciting creations.

Roald Dahl's granddaughter Sophie Dahl is also a writer! She wrote her first book for children in 2019.

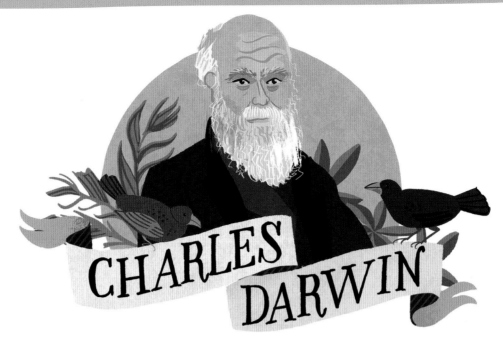

CHARLES DARWIN

When Charles Darwin was born, people in Britain mostly believed that God had made the world, the animals and the people in it just as they are today. The idea of evolution – one species growing and developing out of another – was seen as denying the work of God. Charles's work would later help people understand how life on Earth had changed over thousands of years. But it also made a lot of people very angry!

SECRET SCIENTIST

Charles Darwin was born in Shrewsbury in 1809, the youngest son of Dr Robert Darwin and a wealthy lady called Susannah Wedgwood, who died when he was just eight. After that, his three older sisters looked after him. He wasn't allowed to mention his mother in front of them and had to keep his feelings to himself. Charles looked up to his father, but was also a bit scared of him; his sad, angry moods could fill the house like thunder.

When Charles was at school the boys were supposed to concentrate on learning Latin and Greek, not science. The headmaster thought Charles was foolish for wanting to study chemistry, and his classmates nicknamed him 'Gas'! Not to be put off, Charles and his older brother, Erasmus, carried out scientific experiments by themselves in a shed. Charles also loved to go walking alone, collecting insects and minerals and watching birds.

He had another hobby too – he liked to hunt. When he was a teenager, his father thought he was far too interested in shooting birds like grouse and snipe, and worried that he would waste his life hunting, rather than getting a proper job. So he sent him off, when Charles was just 16, to study medicine at the University of Edinburgh.

Charles took out a lot of library books, but he found the lectures dull, and watching surgery made him feel sick – it was clear that being a doctor wasn't right for him! He carried on hunting and discovered a new hobby: beetle collecting. By now, his father didn't know what to do with his lazy son. Eventually, he decided that being a clergyman would suit Charles better, and sent him to study at Cambridge University instead. Between collecting beetles and studying plants and pollen, Charles managed to pass his exams with very good marks. He imagined a quiet life for himself as a clergyman who loved to study nature.

THE VOYAGE THAT CHANGED EVERYTHING

Then an extraordinary opportunity opened up. A survey ship called the HMS *Beagle* was about to set out on a two-year voyage to South America, and Charles was asked to come along as the ship's naturalist (an expert on the natural world). After eventually winning his father's permission, Charles set sail with the rest of the *Beagle's* crew in 1831.

This voyage changed everything for Charles. Although he was horribly seasick to begin with, he soon recovered and began collecting plankton. In the Cape Verde Islands off the African coast, he saw a layer of seashells high up in a cliff which would have been at sea level thousands of years ago. This proved to Charles that the land was moving and changing all the time. As the *Beagle* sailed along the coast of South America, Charles explored on land, finding plant and animal specimens, fossil-hunting and taking notes to send home. Eventually, the *Beagle* travelled on to the Galapagos Islands, where Charles noticed that the finches on different islands had different kinds of beaks, allowing them to eat different kinds of food. He also visited New Zealand, Australia and the Falkland Islands.

In total, Charles spent five years with the Beagle – even though the voyage was only supposed to last two!

THE ORIGIN OF SPECIES

In 1836, Charles returned to England and began to look over his notes and specimens, thinking about what they showed. Bit by bit, he developed his theory of 'natural selection' – the idea that all species have evolved over thousands of years from the same ancestors. This was completely opposite to what most people thought, but Charles had lots of evidence from his voyage with the HMS *Beagle* to back him up. But it wasn't till 1859 – more than 20 years after his return – that Charles published his book *On the Origin of Species*. He was held up partly by illness, and partly by nervousness about people's angry responses. However, when another scientist, Alfred Wallace, came up with a theory similar to Darwin's, it spurred him on. The two of them published their ideas together in a scientific paper in 1858, and Charles's book appeared the following year. He then published another book, *The Descent of Man*, in 1871, about the evolution of humans.

Charles's books amazed and startled those who read them – and they were talked about everywhere! Many clergymen were horrified. But the ideas that species might change and adapt over time – and that humans had not always looked the same way but evolved from a much earlier form of life – spread like wildfire. Charles had been ill for a lot of the time since he returned from his voyage, and in 1882 he finally died of heart failure. But his life's work had changed the way people thought of evolution forever.

"Intelligence is based on how efficient a species became at doing the things they need to survive."

ELIZABETH I

In Greenwich Palace, 1533, a baby was born to the grandest of parents – the king and queen of England. They didn't celebrate their new arrival – King Henry VIII, desperate for a son, was furious that the baby was a girl. Yet this disappointing daughter would grow up to become one of the most successful rulers in British history. Her name was Elizabeth Tudor, but she would one day be known as 'Gloriana', the 'Virgin Queen' and 'Good Queen Bess'.

THE ROYAL FAMILY

Little Elizabeth's life was sometimes sad and difficult. When she was only two years old, her mother, Anne Boleyn, was beheaded on the orders of her father, so that he could be free to marry again. His new wife, Jane Seymour, soon gave birth to Edward, the son Henry longed for. Elizabeth wasn't treated cruelly, although no one thought she would grow up to take the throne. Catherine Parr, her father's sixth and last wife, was particularly kind to her.

Intelligent and serious, Elizabeth received a royal education from brilliant tutors. She was taught Latin, Greek and history – and she did extremely well at them. It's said that she spoke five languages by the age of 11! As an adult, she could speak or read English, Welsh, Greek, Latin, Spanish, French and Italian.

When Henry VIII died, in 1547, her young half-brother, Edward, became King Edward VI. However, he died just six years later, and things became much worse for Elizabeth because her older half-sister, Mary, took the throne. Though Henry VIII had changed England's religion from Roman Catholic to Protestant, 'Bloody' Mary was determined to make the country Catholic again. She burned and tortured Protestants who wanted to worship differently, and she was convinced that Elizabeth (who was a Protestant) might be plotting to overthrow her. Elizabeth was spied on, questioned and even imprisoned in the Tower of London.

Elizabeth loved sweets, especially candied violets – so much so that many of her teeth went rotten.

TAKING CHARGE

But Elizabeth was clever and cunning, and managed to survive under Mary's eye until her half-sister died, in 1558. At last, Elizabeth became the queen of England. People were happy, but cautious – would Elizabeth be as cruel as Mary? And whom would she marry? Almost everyone expected that Elizabeth's husband would take a big role in ruling the country, so they were anxious about who she would choose. But Elizabeth had no intention of marrying. Wearing expensive, richly jewelled dresses, the beautiful young queen declared that she was married to her kingdom, and set out to create a glamorous, spectacular court with herself at the centre. She surrounded herself with clever, powerful men, but she never married any of them, and she never allowed anyone to forget who was in charge.

Elizabeth knew how to keep attention focused on her. Court ladies were only allowed to wear black or white, so that Elizabeth stood out when she wore bright colours!

WISE RULER

Though Elizabeth spent a lot on her dresses, she was very clever with money when it came to her kingdom; within six years of coming to the throne, she had paid off all the country's debts. During Elizabeth's reign, England became one of the wealthiest countries in Europe. She also told Parliament to pass laws to help resolve the bitter fights between English Protestants and Catholics, which became known as the Elizabethan Religious Settlements. These didn't get rid of religious conflict altogether, but they made it easier for Catholics and Protestants to live side by side.

However, Elizabeth's most famous achievement was the defeat of the Spanish Armada. In 1588, King Philip II of Spain, sent 130 ships carrying 18,000 soldiers to invade England. Elizabeth was praised as a great leader throughout the crisis. When troops were gathered at Tilbury in case the Spanish invaded, she addressed them with a famous speech, in which she announced: "I am come amongst you . . . to lay down for my God, and for my kingdoms, and my people, my honour and my blood even in the dust." Eventually, storms and clever tactics from the English fleet sent the defeated Armada sailing home again.

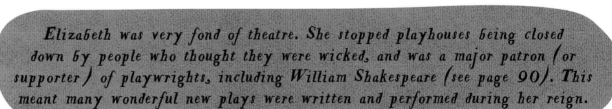

Elizabeth was very fond of theatre. She stopped playhouses being closed down by people who thought they were wicked, and was a major patron (or supporter) of playwrights, including William Shakespeare (see page 90). This meant many wonderful new plays were written and performed during her reign.

A GOLDEN AGE

As Elizabeth grew older, she knew that people would take her less seriously as a queen if she showed any signs of aging or weakness – so she refused to age. She covered up scars from smallpox, which she had survived when she was 29, with thick, lead-based make-up (which may actually have made her more ill). Eventually, though, she was too exhausted by ruling to fight off any more illness. She died, aged 69, in the spring of 1603, as crowds of her grieving citizens filled the streets to mourn her. The Elizabethan Age – stable, peaceful, prosperous and creative – is still considered a 'Golden Age' in British history. Not bad for an unwanted, motherless little girl whom no one thought would ever be queen.

OLAUDAH EQUIANO

Olaudah Equiano, one of the first Black people in Europe ever to publish a book, was born around 1745. Kidnapped and enslaved as a child, he learned to read and write, earned the price of his freedom and became an explorer, before writing his own life story to tell people about the horrors of slavery.

TORN FROM HOME

According to his own autobiography, *The Interesting Narrative of the Life of Olaudah Equiano*, Olaudah was born in the village of Essaka (now in Nigeria), the youngest son of an elder of the Igbo tribe. Olaudah and his older brothers and sister were often left behind to play and guard the village while their parents worked. But this was sometimes dangerous – kidnappers often came to the village, hoping to steal children and sell them into slavery. Olaudah once saved another child by shouting out when he saw a raiding party. However, when he was 11, he and his sister were captured and dragged away themselves. After they were torn from each other, Olaudah would never see his sister or any of the rest of his family again.

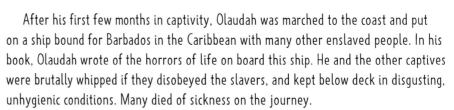

After his first few months in captivity, Olaudah was marched to the coast and put on a ship bound for Barbados in the Caribbean with many other enslaved people. In his book, Olaudah wrote of the horrors of life on board this ship. He and the other captives were brutally whipped if they disobeyed the slavers, and kept below deck in disgusting, unhygienic conditions. Many died of sickness on the journey.

After an awful time at sea, Olaudah was eventually brought to Virginia in North America, where he was sold to a captain in the British navy called Michael Henry Pascal. This captain renamed Olaudah, calling him Gustavus Vassa, and would hit Olaudah if he asked Pascal to use another name.

SEEKING HIS FREEDOM

Pascal travelled widely with Olaudah, bringing him to England, and sending him to school in London to learn to read and write. From time to time, Olaudah had to return to sea with Pascal, because England was fighting a war with France – but he learned the skills of a sailor while on board, which would help him a great deal later on. When the war was over, Olaudah wanted Pascal to give him his freedom. Despite this, Pascal sold him suddenly to another captain, who took him to the Caribbean and sold him on again to a merchant called Robert King.

Here, Olaudah was given a skilled job as a clerk that allowed him to save up £40, the price of his own freedom. Olaudah was finally able to buy his freedom from his enslaver in 1766. By then he had seen terrible things done to enslaved people in the plantation fields, which he would later write about in his autobiography.

He was overwhelmed with happiness to be free again. But he felt passionately that he wanted to help all the other people who were still suffering the misery of slavery.

The Atlantic slave trade lasted over 300 years. During this time, it's estimated that over 12 million people in Africa were taken from their homes, transported overseas and forced into slavery.

THE INTERESTING NARRATIVE

Olaudah went back to sea to earn his living as a merchant and explorer, sailing the Mediterranean and the Atlantic for 20 years. He eventually settled down in England. Here, he married an English woman, with whom he had two daughters and began to write his memoirs. In 1789, with the support of abolitionists – people who campaigned against slavery – his book was published, and became a huge success.

In *The Interesting Narrative of the Life of Olaudah Equiano*, Olaudah told his readers all about the horrors of slavery, the cruel and terrible things he had experienced himself and seen done to others. His book had an enormous impact and became a bestseller. Some people who had assumed that enslaved people somehow could not feel and think as other humans did began to realise how wrong it was to take away their freedom and rights. Olaudah also gave lectures in which he spoke out against slavery and told people about the great harm it did.

Although he died in 1797, 10 years before slavery in Britain was abolished, Olaudah's books and work as an abolitionist made a huge difference to the fight against slavery. His book is still considered incredibly important as one of the earliest stories told by someone who had been enslaved himself.

MO FARAH

Although Mo Farah left Somalia for Britain when he was only a child, and at first found it hard to adapt to his new home, he worked and trained and ran his way to victory, becoming one of the best long-distance runners in the world.

THE TWINS

In 1983, identical twin boys were born to Aisha and Mukhtar Farah in Mogadishu, the capital of Somalia. One brother was called Hassan, the other was called Mohamed – but this soon got shortened to Mo! The twins and their four younger brothers and sisters grew up in the countryside in Somaliland until a war started, and violence tore their home apart. Then Mo and Hassan were sent across the border to the small country of Djibouti, to stay with their grandparents.

Because he was dyslexic, Mo struggled at school, and Hassan had to help him with his reading. He really wanted to be a mechanic, but his family didn't approve of this idea. He was already starting to be good at running, though. When electricity power cuts meant Mo's favourite television show cut out, he'd run to the next street over, then the next, then the next, until he found a street with power – early training for his later victories!

The war in Somalia continued, and, when Mo was eight, he and his two younger brothers were sent overseas to Britain to live with their father, who had been born there. But Hassan was too ill to travel. Mo wouldn't see his beloved twin brother again for 12 whole years.

When he was five or six, Mo was badly burned on his arm in an accident at home. He had a lucky escape, though – if the burn had been a little higher, the nerves in his arm would have been damaged and he might never have been able to run at all.

TIME TO RUN

It took Mo a while to learn English, and he often got into trouble at school because he felt frustrated. He had always loved football, but when he was 11, his PE teacher, Alan Watkinson, suggested he take up running instead. Mr Watkinson drove him to training sessions and encouraged him to work hard. He became such an important figure in Mo's life that when Mo got married in 2010, Mr Watkinson was his best man!

In 1997, Mo won an inter-schools cross-country championship. Four years later, when he was 18, he won the European Junior 5,000 metres, with the help of a new coach, Alan Storey. It was clear now that the little boy who'd struggled to fit in had the potential to become a world-class athlete.

"The atmosphere at the Olympics was incredible; something I've never experienced and will never experience again in my entire life. Running in front of 85,000 people shouting out your name. Wow! It was just unbelievable."

ON THE TRACK TO SUCCESS

Mo continued his training in Kenya and Ethiopia, but he didn't get beyond the semi-finals at his first Olympic Games, in 2008. Determined to do better, he began working with a new coach, and he then won the 5,000-metre race at the World Championships in Daegu, South Korea, in 2011.

Mo was now an incredibly successful runner, at the peak of his fitness. At the London 2012 Olympic Games, with the home crowd cheering wildly for him, he became a double gold medallist, winning both the 5,000-metre and 10,000-metre races.

He went on to repeat his double-gold-winning feat four years later at the 2016 Olympics in Rio de Janeiro, Brazil! After taking gold and silver medals in the 2017 World Championships, Mo switched to running marathons, and won the Chicago Marathon the year after. He was voted BBC Sports Personality of the Year, and was also knighted by the Queen, becoming Sir Mo Farah – and he has won the European Athlete of the Year Trophy three times!

After moving around so much in his early life, and having to say goodbye to homes and family along the way, Mo is now the most successful British track and field athlete of all time. Between 2011 and 2017, he won 10 Olympic and World Championship gold medals!

Mo is known for doing the 'Mobot' – making an M with his arms over his head – to celebrate his victories on the track.

ALEXANDER FLEMING

Born on a remote Scottish farm, Alexander Fleming qualified as a doctor and studied wounds and infection before helping to discover penicillin, the first antibiotic, which would eventually save millions of lives all around the world.

INTELLIGENT BOY

Alexander Fleming – or Alec, as he was usually known – was born in 1881, in Ayrshire, Scotland. Alec grew up on his parents' farm, near a little town called Darvel. He was one of four children – and he had four older half-siblings, too! Their nearest neighbour was a mile away, and he and his brothers and sisters went scrambling through fields and streams, learning from the world around them without knowing they were doing it.

Alec's father died when he was quite young, and his oldest brother, Hugh, took over running the farm. When he was five, Alec went to a tiny little school on the moor, with just one classroom and 12 pupils! After that he went to Darvel School – which meant he had to walk eight miles to and from the town every day. Finally, when his teachers realised how intelligent he was, he was given a scholarship to Kilmarnock Academy, where he boarded for two years. In 1895, he moved to London to live with his brother Tom, who was a doctor. There, he went to a more advanced school called the Regent Street Polytechnic. He was so clever that his teachers quickly moved him into a class with boys who were two years older than him!

Alec was interested in medicine, but his brother encouraged him to go into business to earn money, which he didn't like. However, when Alec's uncle died and left him some money, Tom suggested he put it towards the fees for medical school. Alec worked hard to study for the exams – and passed them with the highest marks of any student in the country! After that, he could choose whichever medical school he liked. Alec studied with a scientist called Sir Almroth Wright, who was researching tiny organisms called bacteria – still a fairly new area of science. He qualified as a doctor and surgeon in 1906, but he didn't begin practising medicine like his brother. Instead, Almroth Wright persuaded him to stay on at the school and help him in his research.

At the age of 25, Alec went to study medicine at St Mary's Medical School, which was part of London University. He went there not because he thought it was the best place to study but because he had played water polo against the St Mary's team!

TREATING INFECTIONS

During the First World War, Alec went to France as part of the Army Medical Corps, where he tried to find better ways of treating wound infections. At that time, people often died from wounds that became infected with bacteria, even if the injury itself wasn't too serious. Alec learned that some of the treatments that were being used to kill bacteria, called antiseptics, did more harm than good to the wounded soldiers. He also found out that a mixture of salt and water could be used to clean large wounds safely.

After the war, he returned to St Mary's to carry on teaching and researching. He discovered that nasal mucus (in other words, snot!) contained natural antiseptic substances, which paved the way for other scientists to discover more about the human body's immune system.

In 1908, Alec earned a gold medal for being the top medical student in the whole university.

DISCOVERING PENICILLIN

But it wasn't until 1928 that he made his greatest, world-changing discovery. Alec was working on an experiment with a bacterium called staphylococcus. The dish containing the bacteria was supposed to be put away, but Alec went off on holiday with his family, leaving the dish uncovered on a bench in the laboratory.

Alec didn't know that a mould called penicillium had got into the dish. When he came back, he saw that mould had grown in his experiment – and that the area where the mould had grown was clear of bacteria. The bacteria had been destroyed by the mould!

Alec did more experiments, but he wasn't able to work out which part of the mould was fighting the infection-causing bacteria. Ten years after Alec's first discovery, two other scientists, Howard Florey and Ernst Chain, finally worked out how to purify it so that doctors could use it on patients. The new drug was called 'penicillin' – one of the first antibiotics ever to be discovered – and it was used during the Second World War to treat the wounded, hugely increasing the number of people who survived their injuries.

In 1945, nearly 20 years after he had found the mould growing, Alec was awarded the Nobel Prize alongside Howard Florey and Ernst Chain. When he died, in 1955, his discovery had already saved countless lives – and people around the world were grateful to him for being so careless in the lab!

PENICILLIN

OWAIN GLYNDŴR

When the last Romans left Britain, in about 400 CE, many Anglo-Saxons came by sea from Germany and Denmark and fought the Britons, whom they called 'the Welsh', for land. These Anglo-Saxon settlers would eventually form the kingdom of England. The Welsh and the English would go on fighting each other for the next 700 years! The very last Welsh person to hold the title of Prince of Wales, and lead the Welsh in a fight for independence, was Owain Glyndŵr.

A NOBLE FAMILY

Owain Glyndŵr was born in 1359, to a powerful family in North-East Wales. His father, Gruffydd, was Prince of a place called Powys – his family had ruled there since before the Normans came to Britain in 1066. His mother, Elen, also came from a noble family. Owain's family owned a lot of land in the Marches, the borderlands between England and Wales. Like other 'Marchers', they moved easily between the Welsh and English worlds, especially when these two worlds were at peace, as they were when Owain was born.

When Owain was still a child, his father died and he was sent to live with Sir David Hanmer, an Anglo-Welsh judge. He was educated in England and followed in Sir David's footsteps by studying law. When he was 24, he married Sir David's daughter Margaret, and then, bored with law and staying at home, he became a soldier. He joined the English army and went to fight for the English King Richard II.

A NEW KING

However, when Richard II was overthrown by Henry IV, things changed for Owain. Henry IV was a harsher ruler than Richard, showing favouritism to the English and treating Welsh nobles like Owain cruelly. People soon became dissatisfied.

Then Reynold, Lord Grey of Ruthin, another lord from the Marches and an old enemy of Owain's, stole some of Owain's lands. The new king took Grey's side, and refused to tell him to give them back. Then Grey deliberately didn't tell Owain that he needed to send some of his own troops to support the king, so Owain found himself unfairly accused of treason.

THE RISE OF THE PRINCE OF WALES

Angry with Grey and King Henry, Owain gave himself the title Prince of Wales and rose in revolt. In September 1400, he began to attack Grey's lands and other towns along the border with England. Henry IV sent the English army to crush Owain, but he failed. Instead, this sparked a rebellion throughout northern and central Wales. Many other Welsh people were inspired to join Owain's cause. Henry tried again and again to stamp out the uprising, but groups of fighters calling themselves *Plant Owain* – 'Owain's Children' – popped up everywhere to attack his soldiers.

Owain won a lot of battles against Henry. In 1401, he captured Conwy Castle, and the next year, at the Battle of Bryn Glas, he defeated the English army and captured its leader, Edmund Mortimer. When Henry refused to pay a ransom to release Edmund, Owain married Edmund to his own daughter, Catrin, creating a strong alliance between the two families.

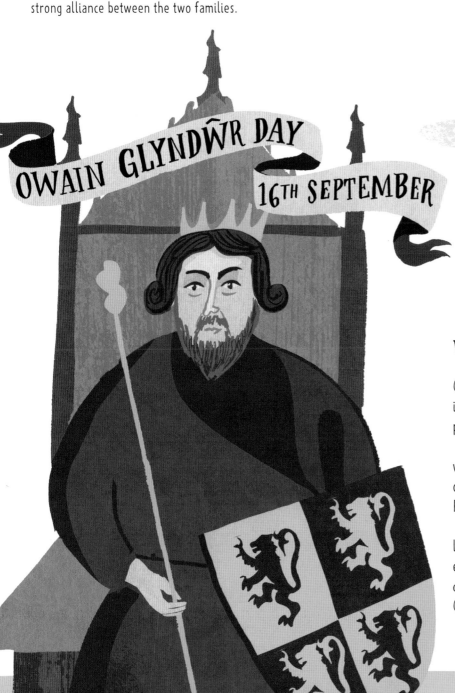

OWAIN GLYNDŴR DAY
16TH SEPTEMBER

All of Owain's sons with Margaret – Gruffudd, Madog, Maredudd, Thomas, John – died in battle or were taken prisoner. None of them had children, so Owain's name died out with them.

WELSH HERO

Owain had big dreams. He had a vision of an independent Wales, with its own universities, church and parliament. He created the first Welsh parliament at Machynlleth in 1404, where he was crowned Prince of Wales.

In the end, though, the lack of a large army prevented Owain achieving what he hoped for Wales. He was never captured, but his rebellion was over in 1409 when his last stronghold, Harlech Castle, was stormed by the English. By 1416, it's believed that he had died in hiding.

After he died, Owain was thought of as a hero in Wales – an almost legendary one, like Robin Hood. Over the years, people told stories of his epic deeds and he is sometimes said, like King Arthur, to be waiting for the day when he is needed to return! He is still celebrated today in Wales on Owain Glyndŵr Day, 16th September.

TANNI GREY-THOMPSON

Born with a condition called spina bifida, Tanni Grey-Thompson is an amazingly successful athlete and a powerful campaigner for the rights of people with disabilities. She is also a TV presenter – and a member of the House of Lords!

NEVER HELD BACK

In the summer of 1969, in Cardiff, Wales, a baby girl was born. She was christened Carys Davina, but when her older sister first saw her, she called her "Tiny" instead. "Tiny" turned to "Tanni" – and that was what the baby's name became!

Tanni had been born with spina bifida, which meant that her spine hadn't developed properly. From the age of seven, she needed to use a wheelchair to get around, but Tanni's parents didn't want that to hold her back. They wanted her to try and achieve whatever she wanted to – their attitude was always "get on with it!" They had to fight for a long time for Tanni to attend a mainstream school, rather than a school for children with disabilities, but both Tanni and her parents were determined that it was where she belonged.

When Tanni was 13, she began wheelchair racing. She represented Wales when she was 15 in the Junior National Wheelchair Games and won the 100-metre race – the first of many, many wins for Tanni.

As well as wheelchair racing, Tanni enjoyed other sports as a child, including horse riding, archery, basketball and swimming.

FIRST MEDAL

When she was still a teenager, Tanni had to have an operation in which a steel rod was used to help straighten her spine. After she recovered, she was determined to compete in bigger races, so she joined a sports club in Cardiff for athletes who used wheelchairs. (Sometimes she and her friends raced each other on the ramps in multi-storey car parks – which was very dangerous!) She was soon in training for the 1988 Seoul Paralympics – and she came home from the competition with her first bronze medal.

RACING CAREER

Tanni had to have another operation on her back after that, which stopped her competing for a year. But when she returned, there was no stopping her. In the Barcelona Paralympics in 1992 she took FOUR gold medals – in the 100 metres, 200 metres, 400 metres and 800 metres!

During her racing career, Tanni won a total of 16 medals, 11 of which were gold medals, at five Paralympic Games between 1988 and 2004. She also won another 12 medals at the World Championships – and won the London Marathon women's wheelchair race six times!

Tanni broke more than 30 world records during her athletic career. She is Britain's greatest ever Paralympic athlete.

"Being in a wheelchair has given me more mobility, not less. It's never stopped me from doing anything I wanted to do."

FINISH

FIGHTING FOR RIGHTS

In 2007, Tanni announced that she was retiring from sport – but she certainly wasn't disappearing from public life. She presented TV programmes, worked with charities, and campaigned for access to sport for people with disabilities. Her quick wit and determination made her as popular and successful on screen as she had been on the track. In recognition of her achievements, she was made first a Dame, and then a Baroness.

In 2013, Tanni gave a speech in Parliament about the ways in which people with disabilities are still often insulted or poorly treated. She talks openly about hurtful or ignorant things that people have said to her and to other people with disabilities, and fights fiercely for their rights, for women and children's rights, and for the people in society who need help and don't get it.

STEPHEN HAWKING

The maths and physics mastermind Stephen Hawking was told, as a young man, that a disease called ALS would hold him back and shorten his life. Instead, Stephen went on studying and asking BIG questions about the universe for more than 50 years!

BORN FOR THE STARS

In the bitter cold of a wartime Oxford winter, on 8th January 1942, a boy called Stephen William Hawking was born, exactly 300 years after the death of the great astronomer Galileo Galilei. His mother, Isobel, had gone to Oxford to have her baby because Germany had promised not to bomb the ancient city, so it was much safer there than in heavily bombed London. A few days before Stephen was born, she bought an atlas of the stars – as if she already knew her baby would grow up to study them.

Stephen's parents were intelligent and well-educated – Isobel had studied at Oxford University, and his father, Frank, was a medical researcher. They had some unusual habits, including driving around in an old taxi! Sometimes young Stephen, his parents and his sisters, Philippa and Mary, would all bring their own books to the dinner table, and everyone would eat and read in total silence.

> Stephen enjoyed taking things apart – although they didn't always go back together again! As a teenager, he built a computer out of clock parts and bits of rubbish with a group of friends.

At school in London, Stephen was quickly nicknamed 'Einstein', although he didn't stand out as a student at first – he was clever, but struggled to focus on lessons and tests in class (and his handwriting was terrible!). But, encouraged by his teacher, he developed a particular interest in maths and he liked to lie outside and look at the stars.

His father thought Stephen should study medicine, so that he could earn more money, but Stephen was drawn to mathematics and physics – he hoped they would allow him to understand more about the laws of the universe. When he was 17, he won a scholarship to study physics and chemistry at Oxford University.

STUDYING THE UNIVERSE

After he graduated, Stephen went on to Cambridge University in 1962, where he studied cosmology – the study of how the universe first came to be and how it might end. However, the year Stephen turned 21, he had some terrible news. Doctors told him that he had a disease called ALS that would gradually take away his ability to move and speak. Many people who got ALS didn't live for very long. Stephen was told he might only have another two years left to live. He felt miserable and depressed. What was the point in continuing his studies?

But Stephen proved the doctors wrong. In 1962, he met Jane Wilde, another student, and fell in love with her. He realised that if he and Jane wanted to get married, he would need to finish studying and get a job – so he did. His brilliance meant he was quickly given a research post at a college, and he would continue to work mostly in Cambridge, studying, teaching, and coming up with new ideas, for the rest of his long life. As he became less mobile, he began to use an electric wheelchair – but he was rather a wild driver! He liked to dance in his chair at parties – and once even crashed and broke his hip while moving at speed.

> From 1979 to 2009, Stephen was the Lucasian Professor of Mathematics at Cambridge – an important post Isaac Newton (page 72) had held in the past, as well as Ada Lovelace's (page 62) mentor Charles Babbage!

ALWAYS QUESTIONS TO ASK

Stephen was particularly interested in the study of black holes, mysterious parts of space where the force of gravity is so strong that nothing can escape from them, not even light. His theories about them – including the idea that they gave off radiation (which would later be called 'Hawking radiation') – helped scientists understand more about these strange objects. He also developed ideas about how the world began and searched for a theory that would explain everything in the universe – though he eventually decided humans could never develop this theory, because they couldn't see all of reality clearly enough. To him, this was a good thing – it meant that there would always be questions to ask.

In 1985 Stephen caught pneumonia on a trip to CERN (the European Centre for Nuclear Research) in Switzerland. The infection nearly killed him, and it left him unable to talk. After that, Stephen spoke with the help of a computer that he worked with a muscle in his cheek.

Stephen wanted his work to be read and understood by everyone, not just scientists. In 1988, his book *A Brief History of Time: From the Big Bang to Black Holes* was published. It has now sold more than 10 million copies!

By the time Stephen died in 2018, at the age of 76 – an incredible 55 years after he was first diagnosed with ALS – he had been awarded a huge number of prizes and medals. He had helped us learn more about the universe we live in and the kinds of questions science can ask – and answer.

> In his autobiography *My Brief History*, Stephen said of his life: "It has been a glorious time to be alive. I'm happy if I have added something to our understanding of the universe."

KELLY HOLMES

Despite setbacks and injuries, the brilliant athlete Kelly Holmes went from driving trucks in the British Army to amazing success on the running track, eventually winning two Olympic gold medals.

SPORTY GIRL

At the start of the 1970s, in a little town called Pembury in Kent, a 17-year-old called Pam had a baby girl. Things were very tough to start with – the baby's father, a mechanic, left before little Kelly was one. Pam's parents suggested she should have Kelly adopted, but Pam loved her daughter and refused to give her up. When Kelly was four, Pam married a painter called Mick Norris, who became Kelly's father – and, after Pam and Mick had two baby boys, their family was complete.

Kelly loved her brothers, treating them like dolls, and they followed her everywhere, wanting to do everything she did. A rough-and-tumble girl, she liked playing with her friends at school, but she didn't work too hard at her lessons – in fact, she was known for mucking about! She was always brilliant at sports, though, and was games captain at her primary school. When she was 12, she joined Tonbridge Athletics Club. Soon, she won the English Schools 1,500-metre race at both junior and senior levels, encouraged by a PE teacher who believed she could succeed in anything. At 14, Kelly wanted to train to be an Olympic champion, but coaching cost a lot of money and Kelly wasn't able to pay for it. So when she was 18, she joined the British Army.

Kelly had other jobs as a teenager. She helped nurse people with disabilities – and also worked as an assistant in a sweet shop!

GO KELLY

TOUGH SERGEANT

At first Kelly was a truck driver, but then became an army fitness instructor. Sergeant Holmes was respected, but known for being tough! After a few years, Kelly decided to return to athletics again, and in 1992 she took up serious training. By 1994, she had won gold in the 1,500 metres at the Commonwealth Games – and was still in the army!

As well as winning races, Kelly was great at volleyball and became the army's female judo champion – she was an amazing all-round athlete.

A FEW SETBACKS

But the next few years were hard for Kelly. Although she set British records for the 800 metres and 1,000 metres in 1995, a fractured bone stopped her winning a medal in the 1996 Atlanta Olympics. Just when she should have been winning international competitions, she had to spend months with her leg in plaster. In 1997, when she finally left the army to devote herself to athletics full-time, she set the UK record for the 1,500 metres – but another serious injury at the Athens World Championships slammed the brakes on again.

However hard she worked to get fitter and stronger, injuries continued to slow Kelly down. Her mental health suffered too – she got very depressed in 2003, just before the World Championships, when she had yet another injury. At the age of 33 – past the peak for many professional athletes – it seemed Kelly's dreams of winning an Olympic gold medal were gone for good.

MAKING HISTORY

But then, at the Athens Olympic Games in 2004, Kelly made history! In an incredibly close race, she won the gold medal in the 800 metres – and, five days later, a second gold in the 1,500 metres! That night, she slept with her medals on her bedside table, unable to believe she had finally realised her childhood dream – and become one of the most successful British track athletes of all time.

Not long afterwards, Kelly was given a damehood by the Queen. Soon after that, she set up the Dame Kelly Holmes Trust, a charity that helps young people facing difficulties in their lives by giving them the chance to be mentored by world-class athletes.

Although she is now retired from professional athletics, Dame Kelly continues to inspire and motivate people – and to run. (But although she is such a brilliant athlete, she hates swimming and really doesn't like getting wet!)

Kelly is now an honorary colonel in the Royal Armoured Corps Training Regiment, making her Colonel Dame Kelly Holmes – the only Colonel Dame in the world.

NOOR INAYAT KHAN

A creative, talented writer and musician, a gentle person who believed in peace and tolerance, Noor Inayat Khan became an unlikely war hero – a spy who worked against the Nazis, and gave her life for her beliefs.

DIFFERENT FROM MOST PRINCESSES

On New Year's Day 1914, in the biting cold of a Moscow winter, Noor-un-Nisa Inayat Khan was born to two very unusual parents. Her mother, Pirani Ameena Begum (born Ora Ray Baker), was an American poet, and her father, Inayat Khan, was an Indian musician and Sufi religious teacher. Noor was of royal blood – she was descended from Tipu Sultan, who ruled the south Indian Kingdom of Mysore in the 18th century – but her life would be very different from those of most princesses.

Not long after her birth, Noor's family moved to London, where they lived in Bloomsbury, an area full of poets, writers and musicians. Little Noor and her younger brothers and sister loved to wander through Gordon Square, a big garden near their house, looking for fairies – which Noor always believed she saw there! When Noor was six, the family moved again to France, to a big house near the city of Paris. The house was always filled with visitors and lights and music, and the children loved it here too. They dressed up in saris and turbans, played outside, gave concerts and put on plays together and looked at the sparkle of Paris in the distance.

When Noor was 13, her father died, leaving the family grieving. For a while, Noor's mother left it to her to look after her brothers and sister, which Noor found hard. She wrote stories and poems to cheer herself up – a habit that stayed with her long after her mother felt stronger. Later, she went to study at a university called the Sorbonne in Paris, as well as learning the harp and the piano – like her father, she was a talented musician. When she finished her studies, she began to write stories again, some of which were published in a French newspaper. Soon her first book, *Twenty Jataka Tales*, was published in English.

A DANGEROUS JOB

But Noor's creative work was interrupted by the outbreak of war. Her father had raised all his children to be peace-loving, in keeping with his religious beliefs. When the Second World War began, however, both Noor and her favourite brother, Vilayat, felt that they must support the fight against Nazi Germany. They left France for London, where Noor volunteered for the Women's Auxiliary Air Force (WAAF). She was one of the first women to be trained as a radio operator . . .

but she was soon to be asked to perform an even more vital – and dangerous – job.

The prime minister, Winston Churchill (page 34), had set up a special secret organisation called the Special Operations Executive (SOE). This trained people who spoke other languages to become spies in Nazi-occupied countries like France, helping people who lived there to resist the Nazis and work against them. After growing up in Paris, Noor spoke perfect, fluent French. The SOE called her in for an interview. They told her that if she took a job with them, she would be in serious danger. Unlike a soldier in uniform, she would have no rights and no protection – if caught, she would be shot. Noor immediately agreed to take the job.

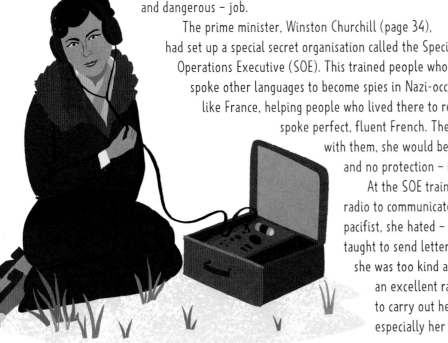

At the SOE training schools, Noor was trained as a wireless operative, who could use a radio to communicate secret messages. She was also taught to handle weapons – which, as a pacifist, she hated – and how to recognise the different uniforms of enemy soldiers. She was taught to send letters in code, and what to do if she was captured. Some of her teachers thought she was too kind and gentle – and sometimes too scatty – to be sent on a mission, but she was an excellent radio operator, and she was needed for the job. Noor herself was determined to carry out her task, although she found it hard to say goodbye to her family - especially her mother.

> *Noor was the first female radio operator to be sent into occupied France. Her code name was 'Madeleine'.*

UNSHAKEABLE COURAGE

In June 1943, Noor landed in north-western France and made her way to Paris. Shortly after she landed, all the other agents in her network were arrested, but she refused to come home, knowing her work sending coded messages was vital. It was desperately dangerous – the Nazis had radio-finding equipment that could track the signal from a wireless transmitter. Noor had to move constantly from place to place, dyeing her hair to disguise herself, and carrying the bulky bag with her equipment. And little did she know it, but she was about to be betrayed to the Nazis by one of her contacts.

In October 1943, just as Noor was about to leave for England, she was captured by the Nazis and sent to a prison in Germany, where she was chained up, kept in solitary confinement and almost starved. She was kept here for almost a year before being taken to Dachau concentration camp, where she was shot. Although she was tortured for information during her imprisonment, she refused to tell her captors anything. In her cell, she invented children's stories to distract herself.

After her death, Noor was awarded the French Croix de Guerre and the British George Cross medals for her courage. A statue of her now stands in Gordon Square, where she used to look for fairies as a little girl.

ELSIE INGLIS

One of the first British women ever to become a doctor, the pioneering medic Elsie Inglis set up hospitals for wounded soldiers during the First World War – that were run and managed only by women!

AN ADVENTUROUS CHILDHOOD

In the foothills of the Himalayas, in 1864, a baby daughter called Elsie was born to John and Harriet Inglis. At that time, India was part of the British Empire, and John Inglis worked for the Indian civil service, helping to govern the country. His job meant that young Elsie and her family – her mother, father and her sister Eva – moved all over India, from the roar and bustle of cities like Calcutta (now Kolkata) to the cool green of the hills.

Elsie grew up adventurous and tough, camping and exploring in the Indian countryside. She was very close to her father, who believed that education was just as important for girls as for boys, which was unusual at the time. Encouraged by him, Elsie wanted to be a doctor from very early on, and painted red spots all over her dolls when they got 'measles'!

Elsie had six older siblings, but they were brought up in England.

INSPIRING AND PERSUASIVE

When Elsie was 12, her father retired from his job, and the family spent two years in Australia before going to live in Scotland. At school in Edinburgh, Elsie was particularly good at history – and she was popular with the other girls, especially when she managed to win the right for the girls to play outside in the square for exercise! Even as a young girl, she had a strong character, and the knack of persuading and inspiring people. Elsie was sent to Paris for one last year of school when she was 18, and then she came back to Edinburgh, eager to begin learning again.

However, not long after she came back from Paris, her mother died of scarlet fever, so she spent some years taking care of her father and running the household. Finally, in 1886, Elsie was able to start studying at the Edinburgh School of Medicine for Women. This new school had just been opened by Dr Sophia Jex-Blake, who had been one of the first women ever to study medicine at university.

FIGHTING FOR WOMEN'S CARE

Dr Jex-Blake was very strict, and some of her students disagreed with her rules, including Elsie. Three years later, with her father's help, Elsie set up her own rival Edinburgh College of Medicine for Women and continued her training there. In 1892, at the age of 27, she qualified as a doctor.

Dr Elsie Inglis was always interested in the poorest patients, and those most in need of care. The more she saw how women were treated, the angrier she felt. She joined the fight for women's suffrage (the right to vote), travelling around Britain to organise meetings. She set up a hospital where poor women could give birth to their babies, and often didn't charge patients if they couldn't pay. Sometimes, she even used her own money to pay to send patients to the seaside to recover!

THE SCOTTISH WOMEN'S HOSPITALS

In 1914, the First World War began, and soon huge numbers of wounded soldiers desperately needed medical care. Elsie went to the War Office to volunteer her services, but she was rudely dismissed with the words: "My good lady, go home and sit still." However, Elsie was not put off so easily. She decided to organise independent hospital units run by women. To do this, she would need a lot of money – but when she advertised and ran meetings, donations poured in, and this allowed her to create the Scottish Women's Hospitals for Foreign Service (SWH).

France and Serbia were only too pleased to welcome the SWH. Elsie went to Serbia in 1915 as the Chief Medical Officer with her unit, and worked hard to reduce infection and improve conditions and hygiene in the hospitals she tended. Several of her colleagues died of a terrible illness called typhus, but the work they did there was never forgotten.

When Germany invaded Serbia, Elsie was imprisoned and then sent home, but she returned in 1916 to help the Serbs in Russia. She stayed there until they were forced to leave again the next year. She knew then that she was dying of cancer, but she sent a very cheerful message back to Scotland anyway: "On our way home. Everything satisfactory, and all well except me." She died the day after the boat landed, mourned by many, including the thousands of French, Serbian and Scottish patients she had helped.

Elsie was the first woman to receive the Order of the White Eagle, the highest honour for heroism in Serbia.

JUDITH KERR

If you've ever heard a *Mog* story, or read *The Tiger Who Came to Tea*, you've enjoyed the work of Judith Kerr, whose funny, gentle picture books have delighted millions of children all around the world.

A CHILDHOOD ON THE MOVE

Judith was born Anne Judith Kerr in 1923, in Berlin, Germany's elegant capital city. Her parents, Alfred, a writer, and Julia, a musician, were clever and artistic. From when she was very young, Judith loved to draw and paint. But Judith's family were forced to leave Germany when she was only nine. They were in danger – the Kerrs were Jewish, and Alfred had criticised the Nazis, a political group who hated Jewish people. When Alfred heard that the Nazis were about to take charge and he would be arrested, he fled to Switzerland, followed by Julia and the children. From Switzerland, they went to France, and eventually on to England, where they were safe at last from the invading Nazis. (Judith would later write about what it was like to have to escape to a new country in her book *When Hitler Stole Pink Rabbit*.)

Judith and her brother, Michael, learned French and English easily. However, settling into new places was harder for their parents. As refugees, the Kerrs had to live in a hotel room, relying on charity and help from friends, without a proper home of their own. It was difficult for Alfred to find work, and he and Julia missed their old life – but they had escaped the Nazis. Judith was always grateful that her family had found refuge in Britain. Although she felt like an outsider at times – she went to 10 different schools during her childhood – she still loved making quick, colourful sketches everywhere she went. She was a huge perfectionist, though – sometimes she felt like she rubbed out more lines than she drew.

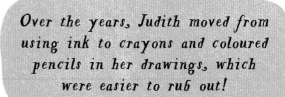
Over the years, Judith moved from using ink to crayons and coloured pencils in her drawings, which were easier to rub out!

THE TIGER ARRIVES

During the Second World War, Judith left school and volunteered with the Red Cross, sorting bandages for wounded soldiers. When the war was over, she went back to her drawing, winning a scholarship to the Central School of Arts and Crafts, and then teaching art at a school. After that, she joined the BBC as a scriptwriter and met another scriptwriter called Nigel Kneale, whom she married in 1954. When they moved into a house with a garden, Judith immediately got a cat – something she'd wanted to do for years!

Judith and Nigel had two children, Tacy and Matthew. Judith gave up her job to look after them, which she sometimes found boring. But Tacy and Judith loved the tigers in the zoo, which they often went to visit. To entertain Tacy at bedtime one day, Judith made up a story about a little girl, her mother and a visiting tiger who ate up all the food in the house. Five years later, when Tacy was at school, she began to turn it into a book, drawing the pictures herself. She remembered all the words easily, because Tacy had made her tell it so many times! In 1968, *The Tiger Who Came to Tea* was published for the first time and became an instant success. It has now sold more than five million copies.

When Nigel wrote his most famous show, The Quatermass Experiment, Judith helped him create special effects for the monster in the show by gluing leaves onto gloves!

There was usually a cat sitting on Judith's lap while she was working. Her ninth cat, Katinka, also featured in one of her books, Katinka's Tail.

THE STORY OF MOG

Judith went on to write many more books, usually based on her day-to-day family life. One was the story of *Mog the Forgetful Cat*, about a cat who forgets how to get into her house and catches a burglar by mistake – this was based on Judith's naughty tabby cat, who wouldn't use the cat flap. This book, and many other stories about Mog – including one in which Mog dies, *Goodbye Mog*, which Judith wrote to help children say goodbye to loved pets – became very popular too. Their gentle humour delighted both young children and grown-ups, and her rounded, colourful pictures were warm and cosy enough to sink into.

When Judith died in 2019, at the age of 95, she had written more than 30 books, selling over 10 million copies around the world. She was still working and talking about her books, and had just published a new one, *The Curse of the School Rabbit*. The little girl who narrowly escaped the Nazis had become one of the best-loved British children's authors of all time, bringing joy to families everywhere.

ADA LOVELACE

Though Ada Lovelace was born at a time when women weren't expected to be good at maths or science, her brilliant mind and original thinking would one day see her called "the first computer programmer".

GIFTED GIRL

When a wild, moody man of letters got married to a religious, highly educated society lady, it's not surprising things didn't end well. The famous poet Lord Byron married Anne Isabella Milbanke in January 1815. Their daughter, Augusta Ada Byron, known as Ada, was born in December.

Ada's family life was strange and difficult. Her parents' marriage was unhappy and they split up when Ada was only a month old. Her father never saw his wife or child again, dying when Ada was only eight. Ada's mother didn't care very much for her daughter either. Young Ada was mainly looked after by servants and her grandmother – and by her pet cat, Mistress Puff!

However, one thing Anne did insist on was that her daughter should be taught a lot of maths. Anne herself was good with numbers – in fact, Lord Byron had called her his "Princess of Parallelograms"! – and she thought that scientific subjects would help stop Ada from becoming like her moody, rebellious father. So Ada was taught maths from the age of four – very unusual for a girl of that time. She turned out to be even better at maths than her mother (although she was still sometimes moody and rebellious).

Ada grew up clever and inventive, keen to examine things and to figure out what made them work. When she was 12, she studied birds and came up with a plan for a flying machine in the form of a winged horse, powered by steam! She called her study of flight 'flyology'.

Ada became very ill with measles when she was 13, and had to stay in bed for nearly three years. It took a long time for her to recover completely, and she had to walk with crutches for months. Eventually, though, she got well enough to do all the things that wealthy young girls were supposed to – including being presented to the king!

A MEETING OF MINDS

When Ada was 17, she met the mathematician Charles Babbage, who would become her lifelong mentor. Charles had invented an early form of the calculator called a 'Difference Engine'. It was a big machine made of brass, which inspired Ada as soon as she saw it. Charles was equally charmed by Ada and her brilliant mathematical mind.

In 1835, when Ada was 19, she met William, Lord King, and the two of them were married later that year. When William was made an earl, Ada became the Countess of Lovelace. Though Ada was kept busy looking after her home and her three children, born between 1836 and 1839, she soon longed to take up her studies again.

Charles Babbage, meanwhile, was working on a new 'Analytical Engine' – an early kind of computer. Ada was just as fascinated by Charles's new invention as she had been by his first. When she was 26, she translated a French article about Charles's Analytical Engine into English and added her own notes – which were three times as long as the article itself! In these notes, Ada wrote about how the machine could be programmed with a code so that it would carry out calculations. Because of this, she is widely recognised as the world's first computer programmer. (She also corrected what Charles called "a grave mistake" in his own calculations – making her the world's first debugger, as well!)

A portrait of Ada by Margaret Sarah Carpenter hangs in 10 Downing Street, where the British prime minister lives. Ada always hated it because it made her jaw look so big!

PROPHET OF THE COMPUTER AGE

Ada was a true visionary. Charles thought that his Analytical Engine, if it was ever built, would only be used for calculating numbers – but Ada imagined that the machine could code music, control processes in a factory, even allow people to communicate – all things that computers can do today. Though she had a gift for maths and calculation, it was Ada's imagination that made her extraordinary, and her refusal ever to stop asking questions and being curious. She always considered her work "poetical science" – the perfect combination of her father's literary brilliance and her mother's gift for numbers.

Ada's health failed shortly after she finished her pioneering work on the Analytical Engine. She died in 1852 at the age of only 36, and was buried beside the father she never knew. Although her work wasn't valued in her lifetime, today she is remembered as 'the prophet of the computer age'.

Like her legacy, Ada's name lives on today. She is remembered every October on Ada Lovelace Day, and the United States Department of Defense has a computer language called 'Ada'!

PAUL McCARTNEY

When the teenage Paul McCartney met a boy called John Lennon, neither of them dreamed that the music they'd make together would become famous all around the globe. With George Harrison and Ringo Starr, Paul and John became the Fab Four – also known as the Beatles!

ROCK 'N' ROLL BABY

James Paul McCartney was born in Liverpool in 1942. His father, Jim, wasn't impressed at first – the new baby was all red-faced and made horrible squawking noises! Little did his dad know that this noisy baby would grow up to be one of the most famous musicians in the world.

Paul's father was also a musician, although he now worked as a salesman – he'd played jazz piano with a local band, and he loved show tunes, which inspired Paul later too. Paul's mother, Mary, who was a midwife, died when Paul was only 14. He and his younger brother, Mike, depended on their dad, who supported his sons and encouraged them to work hard for what they wanted. Music – playing it and listening to it – also helped Paul deal with his grief. He liked American rock'n'roll artists like Little Richard and Buddy Holly.

Keen to help, Jim gave the teenage Paul a trumpet for his birthday – but he soon swapped it for a guitar, so he could sing and play at the same time! On the old piano in the front room, Paul learned to thump out songs – he never had music lessons, but he had a good ear and an instinct for finding the right notes. And he was a born performer.

When Paul thought about what he might do for a living, his father advised him to become a teacher – but at that point, Paul really wanted to be a long-distance truck driver!

MAKING THE BEATLES

When Paul was 15, he met a boy called John Lennon at a church festival, playing in a band called the Quarrymen, and impressed him with his skill on the guitar. Eventually, John asked Paul to join the band. They played a combination of rock'n'roll and a kind of music called 'skiffle', which was a mix of jazz, folk and blues. George Harrison, a younger friend of Paul's, also joined, in 1958. After this, they changed their name a few times before coming up with the Beatles. They began to play more and more shows, at clubs in Liverpool and then in Hamburg, Germany. When their drummer left, in 1962, they replaced him with Ringo Starr and the legendary line-up was finally complete!

When he first heard them play "She Loves You", Paul's father suggested John and Paul should change the lyrics from "Yeah, Yeah, Yeah" to "Yes, Yes, Yes"! They didn't take his advice . . .

HIT AFTER HIT

The band released their first album, *Please Please Me*, in 1963. After that, 'Beatlemania' began to take over the world, as the band racked up hit after hit, from "Love Me Do" and "I Want to Hold Your Hand" to "A Hard Day's Night". Their singles and albums soon sold thousands of copies worldwide. When the Beatles appeared, in their trademark 'moptop' matching haircuts and sharp suits, their fans shrieked and mobbed them! As the band developed musically, they changed their look and sound, making albums with different influences, like *Rubber Soul*, *Revolver*, *Sgt. Pepper's Lonely Hearts Club Band* and *Magical Mystery Tour*.

Even today, The Beatles are the bestselling musical act of all time.

THE MUSIC NEVER STOPPED

But by the time the Beatles released *The Beatles* (also known as *The White Album*) in 1968, there were tensions in the band – all of its members wanted different things. After one last show in 1969, the group broke up, and its members began to make music on their own. Paul formed a group called Wings with his wife, Linda, releasing albums like *Band on the Run* and *Wings at the Speed of Sound*, which were hugely successful.

The Beatles never reunited. Ten years later, in 1980, John was tragically shot and killed, and George died of cancer in 2001. Paul's wife also died of cancer in 1998. But Paul never stopped making music, playing concerts or experimenting with sound. In fact, he released a new album in 2020, at the age of 78!

Over the whole of his career, Paul has sold 100 million copies of his singles!

IAN McKELLEN

The actor and activist Ian McKellen is best known for playing Gandalf the wizard in *The Lord of the Rings*. As well as winning awards and thrilling audiences, Ian has campaigned for the rights of LGBT+ people for many years.

A LOVE OF THEATRE

In May 1939, a few months before the Second World War broke out, Ian Murray McKellen was born in Burnley, a mill town in the north of England. His family soon moved to nearby Wigan, where Ian loved watching the traders shouting in Market Square – their playful patter showed the little boy how powerful acting performances could be, even selling apples! He also loved listening to his father, Denis, play the piano when he was in bed.

But Ian's early life wasn't always cosy – Britain was now at war, and he and his family were often afraid that bombs would fall on their home. Five-year-old Ian slept under a bomb-proof steel table, and all the windows had to be blacked out in case a glimmer of light showed an enemy plane where to target.

Despite the restrictions of wartime, Ian and his older sister, Jean, grew up loving the theatre, just like their mother, Margery. When Ian was nine, his parents gave him a folding toy theatre for Christmas, with cardboard scenery for famous plays like *Cinderella* and *Hamlet*, which could be moved with wires. At school, his English teacher often cast him in plays, especially in the miniature theatre where the boys put on shows once a term. Ian also went on school summer camps to Stratford-upon-Avon. Here, he would queue overnight for cheap tickets to see some of the greatest actors alive – even though that meant he sometimes fell asleep during the show!

At school, Ian and his friends were completely 'stage-struck', and would startle other boys by acting out scenes in the playground!

FROM STUDENT TO WIZARD

After he left school, Ian won a scholarship to study English at Cambridge University – but he acted in so many plays as a student that his scholarship was taken away! However, critics were beginning to notice his talent, and he now knew that he wanted to be an actor and nothing else. In 1961, he made his first professional appearance in a play.

Over the next 30 years, he steadily became a more successful and well-loved theatre actor, especially in Shakespearean plays (page 90). He played the lovestruck Romeo, the villainous Richard III and the powerful enchanter Prospero. And he even played a pantomime dame in *Aladdin*!

In the 1990s, Ian began to take on more film roles, and in the 2000s, he gave his best-known performances of all: Gandalf the wizard in *The Lord of the Rings*, and the metal-controlling Magneto in the *X-Men* films.

Ian has won many awards for acting, including six Olivier Awards, a Tony Award and a Golden Globe. He has also been nominated for two Oscars and four BAFTAs.

ACCEPTANCE WITHOUT EXCEPTION

But acting isn't the only thing Ian is known for. Before 1967, it was illegal for men in Britain to be gay. Even after the law was changed, another law called Section 28 was introduced in 1988, making it illegal to 'promote homosexuality' – for example, by teaching children that some families might have two mums or two dads. This law made it very hard for LGBT+ children to find support.

At that time, in an interview on the radio, Ian 'came out', and told people that he was gay himself. Because he was so well known, his honesty helped many others, although Ian did it because he felt he couldn't keep hiding: "The minute I came out, I felt immediately better in every way . . . I felt relieved that I wasn't lying." At the age of 48, he had become an activist. He went on to co-found Stonewall, a powerful charity organisation that campaigns for LGBT+ rights, whose slogan is 'Acceptance without exception.'

While he may not actually be able to do magic or control metal with his mind, Ian has used his two super-powers, acting and activism, to entertain, inspire and encourage millions of people. Thinking about his greatest achievements, he has said that his gravestone should say: "Here lies Gandalf. He came out"!

YEHUDI MENUHIN

The amazing violinist Yehudi Menuhin was born in New York, travelled the world playing with famous orchestras and settled in Great Britain, where he set up a school for other brilliant young musicians.

OBSESSED WITH THE VIOLIN

In 1916, a Russian Jewish couple, Moshe and Marutha, arrived in New York City in the United States. While looking for somewhere to live, they met a landlady who didn't like Jewish people. Not long after this, their first child was born. Defiantly, they named their little boy Yehudi, meaning 'The Jew'.

From the age of three, Yehudi was obsessed with the violin. When he heard Louis Persinger, the leader of the San Francisco Symphony Orchestra, playing, he demanded a violin of his own. But when he was given a toy tin violin for his birthday, he threw it away, complaining that it didn't sing! Shortly after that, he was given a real violin and began to have lessons with Louis Persinger himself. He was incredibly talented and learnt very quickly, playing his first public concert with Louis at the age of just seven.

When Yehudi was four, his sister Hephzibah was born. A year later, another sister, Yaltah, followed. Both sisters grew up to be talented pianists – and Hephzibah became Yehudi's favourite accompanist.

GOLD STANDARD CONCERTO

Yehudi and his two sisters were never sent to school. They studied at home with their parents – who were strict teachers and insisted on a lot of learning! After Yehudi's first concert, lots of people wanted to hear him play, and the family travelled to many different places to allow him to perform. He went to study in Paris, France, with the Romanian composer and violinist Georges Enesco. Yehudi became very fond of Georges and worked with him all his life.

In 1927, when Yehudi was 11, he played Beethoven's "Violin Concerto" at the well known Carnegie Hall in New York. All of a sudden, he was famous! After that, he toured concert halls around the world, playing music by composers like Brahms, Mozart, Bach and many others. In 1932, Yehudi, aged 16, played the English composer Edward Elgar's "Violin Concerto" – with Elgar, aged 75, conducting! This recording is still thought of as the perfect version of this concerto, against which all other performances are judged.

THE POWER OF MUSIC HEALS

During the Second World War, Yehudi played to Allied troops who were fighting against Nazi Germany. Later on, accompanied by a pianist called Benjamin Britten (who would become a famous composer too), he played to survivors of the Belsen concentration camp in Germany. Over 50,000 people – mostly Jewish people – had died there during their imprisonment by the Nazis. After the Nazis had been defeated and the war was over, Yehudi was also the first Jewish musician to visit Germany to play with the Berlin Philharmonic Orchestra. Some people criticised him for doing this, but Yehudi, who believed in the power of music to heal, felt strongly that it was the right thing to do to help bring people back together.

Yehudi had felt attracted to Great Britain since discovering the music of Elgar, and in 1959, he settled in London. In 1963, he set up the Yehudi Menuhin School in Surrey, England, to help teach musically gifted children with talent like his own. Here, he taught many brilliant pupils, some of whom grew up to become famous musicians too.

> *After Yehudi had played a concert, he liked to end the evening by eating an ice cream. His favourite flavour was strawberry!*

A WEALTH OF WONDERFUL RECORDINGS

Throughout his life, Yehudi was outspoken when he thought people in power were doing the wrong thing. He spoke out against 'apartheid' in South Africa, which was a set of laws that kept people of different skin colours apart and gave white people more power. He also said the bad treatment of people who criticised the Russian government was wrong. This didn't always make his life easy, but he never stopped doing it.

Yehudi loved the Western classical composers he'd grown up with, but he was also adventurous and keen to experience other types of music. He enjoyed playing jazz music, and exploring Indian music with the famous sitar player Ravi Shankar. In India, he also fell in love with yoga, which he practised daily for the rest of his life.

As he grew older, the arm he used to hold his violin bow became weaker, so he did more conducting than performing, leading many of the world's most famous orchestras. He was made first Sir Yehudi, then Lord Menuhin, but he preferred to be known just as Yehudi.

Yehudi died in 1999, leaving behind hundreds of wonderful recordings – and the joyful memories of his students and the people who had heard his extraordinary performances.

> *In 1982, Yehudi conducted Beethoven's Fifth Symphony for the Berlin Philharmonic Orchestra's 100th anniversary gala – standing on his head, and conducting with his feet!*

FREDDIE MERCURY

A shy boy who loved music and stamp collecting, Farrokh Bulsara grew up to
become the unforgettable performer Freddie Mercury, lead singer of Queen,
whose amazing songs would live on long after his death.

FROM FARROKH TO FREDDIE

Farrokh Bulsara was born in 1946, in Zanzibar, which is a part of East Africa now called Tanzania.
His parents, Bomi and Jer, were Parsis – people of Persian heritage, who follow a religion called
Zoroastrianism. Farrokh was brought up in the same faith, which stayed important to him all his life.
The family moved to India not long after Farrokh was born, and he and his sister, Kashmira,
grew up there, near the huge city of Bombay (now called Mumbai).

Farrokh started learning to play the piano at the age of seven.
He fell in love with making music early on – one of his school
friends said later that he could play any song he heard straight
away! When he was a bit older, he started using the name
Freddie – and at the age of 12, he formed his very first band,
which played covers of classic rock and roll songs. Calling
themselves The Hectics, they wore skinny string ties and
styled their hair in big 'puffs'. Freddie also collected
stamps, a hobby he shared with his dad.

*Freddie's voice was amazingly
powerful – and the range of
notes he could sing spanned
four whole octaves. Most people
have a range of two! Freddie
believed this was because he had
four extra teeth in his mouth
– something which made him
self-conscious about his smile
all his life.*

In 1963, when Freddie was 17, the family moved back to Zanzibar.
But when a revolution swept the country, they had to flee, this
time to England. The Bulsaras moved to Middlesex, where Freddie
studied art and graphic design. He didn't forget his love of music,
though. He soon joined up with a local band called Ibex, and then
one called Sour Milk Sea, with whom he started singing some of
his own songs. He eventually had to move out of his parents' house
because the neighbours complained about the noise!

QUEEN TAKES TO THE STAGE

Then Freddie met two people who would help him create truly world-changing music: a guitar player called Brian May and a drummer called Roger Taylor, both members of a band named Smile. When the lead singer of Smile left in 1970, Freddie, aged 24, took over from him – and got the band to change their name to Queen. At about the same time, he changed his own surname from Bulsara to Mercury. The next year, the band was joined by the bassist John Deacon, and Queen's line-up was complete.

Queen's first album, just called *Queen*, and their second, *Queen II*, didn't sell many copies, but the band still carried on making music, and went on to become incredibly successful. Ten years after Freddie joined the band, tens of thousands of fans were packing stadiums to see them perform, desperate to hear songs like :"We Will Rock You", "We Are The Champions", "Another One Bites the Dust", "I Want to Break Free" and "Bohemian Rhapsody".

Freddie loved cats – so much so that he kept 10 of them, giving them names like Goliath, Tiffany and Romeo. Every cat got a Christmas stocking, filled with treats and toys – and in 1985 Freddie even dedicated an album to one of them!

UNFORGETTABLE PERFORMER

Freddie's extraordinary voice, flamboyant performing style and outrageous stage personality combined with Brian May's amazing guitar skills to wow their audiences. Freddie wore outfits like angel wings, silver-sequinned leotards, harlequin suits and royal robes during shows. Although he was shy in daily life, he moved about the stage with incredible flair, delighting the crowds with his performances.

Although he never talked publicly about it, Freddie had relationships with both men and women. During the 1980s, many people, especially gay men, died of an illness called AIDS. Freddie announced that he had the disease in 1991. He died the next day, at the tragically young age of 45 – but leaving behind a musical legacy that would never be forgotten. His assistant said he had just one regret: "that he still had music in him".

Queen's most famous song, "Bohemian Rhapsody", is nearly six minutes long! The band was told it could never be a hit when they wanted to release it, but it became their most popular track. It is often voted the greatest song ever made!

ISAAC NEWTON

A lonely little boy from an ordinary farming family, Isaac Newton grew up to become the greatest mathematician of his generation, famous for discovering the laws of gravity, for splitting white light into the colours of the rainbow, and for his three laws of motion.

LEFT BEHIND

Though civil war was raging in England, the little village of Woolsthorpe in Lincolnshire remained a quiet, sleepy place. In January 1643, a tiny baby was born there, much earlier than expected. He was so small and frail that he wasn't expected to live longer than one day – and he had already lost his father, who'd died three months before he was born. His mother, Hannah Ayscough, waited a week before having him baptised Isaac.

When Isaac was three, his mother had to leave him with his grandparents to get married again – to a wealthy vicar called Barnabas Smith, who didn't want a stepchild around. Being left behind in this way had a deep effect on Isaac, and he hated his stepfather because of it – he once threatened to burn down the house over his head!

Isaac's stepfather died in 1653, but Isaac went to live with an apothecary (someone who prepared and sold medicines) called Clark so that he could attend a grammar school in Grantham. He learned to read Latin here, but his school reports said he was lazy and didn't pay attention! Many stories were told about Isaac at school, though – that he flew kites lit with candle-lanterns at night, and that he made models of sundials, mouse-operated mills and even an early go-kart! His mother tried to take him out of school to look after the family land, but Isaac hated farming, and his uncle and headteacher persuaded Hannah that he should go back to school and then on to university.

There's a story that when Isaac was supposed to be watching sheep, he would study or make models of watermills instead, letting the sheep wander off into other people's fields!

When Isaac started studying colour and the rainbow, he divided it into five colours at first – but he added orange and indigo later, because the ancient Greek mathematician *Pythagoras* had said that seven was a magical number!

THE YEAR OF WONDERS

Isaac went to the University of Cambridge as a 'subsizar' – someone who worked as well as studying, in order to pay some of his fees. He began by studying law, but he soon began teaching himself mathematics. He was also interested in optics (the behaviour of light) and astronomy (the study of stars, planets and other objects in the universe).

After Cambridge University was closed by the plague, Isaac had to return home. But he didn't give up his studies, or his experiments. Between 1665 and 1667, also known as his 'Year of Wonders', he developed the theory of uniform circular motion – the way a planet moves when it orbits a star, or the way the hands of a watch go round – and he discovered calculus, a kind of maths that helps us calculate answers from numbers that are continually changing.

Isaac loved telling the story to his friends of how, as a young student, he saw an apple fall from a tree in the orchard, and wondered why apples always fall straight down, rather than in different directions. This observation led him to develop his law of universal gravitation, or gravity.

COUNTLESS DISCOVERIES

In 1669, Isaac became the first person in the world to build a reflecting telescope.

When he went back to Cambridge in 1667, he was made a Fellow, and then, two years later, Professor of Mathematics.

In 1687, he published his most important book, the *Principia*, which contained his three laws of motion – describing how an object can be expected to move when different forces act on it – as well as his theory of gravity. The *Principia* had a huge effect on science and scientific thinking, even though not everyone always accepted or agreed with what Isaac had written.

After that, Isaac switched his attention away from science. He became a Member of Parliament (MP) in 1689. He was appointed Master of the Mint, in charge of improving the quality of the money people used and punishing people who were making fake coins. In 1705, he was made a knight by Queen Anne.

Isaac argued with lots of people, especially other scientists like Robert Hooke, who was his rival. He could be very difficult to deal with. But he also acknowledged that he owed a lot to thinkers who came before him: "If I have seen further, it is by standing on the shoulders of giants."

When he died, in 1727, at the age of 84, he had made countless discoveries that changed how we see the world and how we understand it. Today we still measure force in 'Newtons'.

PHILOSOPHIÆ NATURALIS PRINCIPIA MATHEMATICA

FLORENCE NIGHTINGALE

Florence Nightingale's family wanted her to become a rich man's wife – but instead, she helped to shape modern nursing, saved the lives of many wounded soldiers, and became known as the "Lady with the Lamp".

FROM FLORENCE TO HAMPSHIRE

In the early 19th century, a rich young couple called William and Frances Nightingale enjoyed a long European honeymoon. It was so long that not one, but two daughters were born during their travels! Their second child was born in 1820, in the Italian city of Florence, and named after her birthplace.

In 1821, the babies and their parents travelled back to England, where Florence and her sister, Frances Parthenope, were brought up on their big family estates in Derbyshire and Hampshire. Florence was very clever, and her father taught her subjects like Latin, history and maths – lessons that were usually taught only to boys.

Meanwhile, their mother wanted her daughters to be graceful and ladylike, to marry wealthy men and make their family look good. Florence did not agree. This was not what she wanted for her life, and she had a lot of arguments about it with her mother.

When Florence was 16, she had what she believed was a call from God, telling her to look after other people. To her parents' horror, she told them she wanted to study nursing. At the time, this wasn't considered a suitable job for wealthy young women, who were supposed to focus on looking beautiful and finding good husbands! Though Florence had looked after sick relatives and other poorly people living on her father's estates, her parents said she couldn't become a nurse.

Florence's elder sister was also named after the place where she was born – Parthenope. Her nickname was "Pop"!

As well as her nursing work, Florence also found time to write a book – a novel called *Cassandra*. In it, she talked about how educated women were wasted on boring family duties, when they could contribute so much more if they were allowed out into the world!

CARING FOR THE SICK

On a trip to France in 1838, Florence met a woman very unlike her mother. Defiant and unconventional, the independent Mary Clarke believed that men and women could be equals. She inspired Florence so much that the two would stay friends for the rest of their lives. Florence's determination to help others, and also to make her own way in life, was renewed. In 1851, she enrolled at a hospital in Germany to study nursing.

In 1853, Florence took a job at a care home for sick women. Her work impressed her employers so much that she was soon put in charge. Using the skills she'd learned, she worked hard to improve hygiene and care. She was good at analysing figures and statistics too, which helped her to notice what kinds of treatment made her patients better more quickly, and so reduce infections.

While she was travelling in Athens, Florence rescued a baby owl from children who were tormenting it. She called it Athena, after the Greek goddess of wisdom. The little owl went everywhere with Florence and liked to sit on her shoulder or in her pocket.

LADY WITH THE LAMP

The following year, Britain joined the Crimean War against Russia, and Florence faced the greatest challenge of her life. Hearing that wounded soldiers were suffering under terrible conditions, she asked the Minister for War to send her out to help. She went out to Scutari in Turkey with her team of nurses, where injured British soldiers were being treated. Here she found a filthy hospital overrun with rats, with blocked toilets and no clean water supplies. Patients had to sleep on the floor, without beds or even blankets.

Calling for money from home, Florence ordered repairs and improvements, and installed proper beds and plumbing. Many of her patients quickly began to recover. Because she visited their beds at night, making sure that they were comfortable, Florence became known as "the Lady with the Lamp". She was soon considered a heroine, both in Scutari and at home – Queen Victoria herself wrote to thank her for her work.

After the war, Florence's own health was poor – in fact, she spent a lot of the next 40 years in bed – but she continued to write about how to improve hospitals and train nurses. In 1860, she founded the new Nightingale Training School for Nurses at St Thomas' Hospital in London. Inspired by Florence, many women were eager to enrol. Today, Florence is thought of as the founder of modern nursing.

CHRIS PACKHAM

The TV presenter Chris Packham is a much-loved wildlife expert, author and campaigner, who has educated both adults and children about animals and the importance of conservation for the whole of his career.

LOVING THE NATURAL WORLD

Chris was born in Southampton in 1961. From the moment he could crawl, it was clear Chris loved wild creatures and the natural world more than anything. He kept ladybirds and beetles in jam jars in his room, and studied the dinosaur pages of encyclopaedias. He loved tropical fish and reptiles and spent hours in the local pet shop, staring into cages and tanks. He thought all the time about the ways that animals lived, behaved and died. When he was 14, Chris found a wild kestrel chick. He called it Kem and cared for it as it grew up, letting it out every day. When it became ill and died, he was heartbroken. He still remembers the kestrel, and remains fascinated by birds of prey.

As a little boy, Chris desperately wanted a bat – so much so that he called his pet mouse Batty!

SEEING THE WORLD IN DETAIL

Chris has Asperger syndrome, a form of autism, which means that he sees, hears and feels the world differently to some other people. At secondary school, he was badly bullied when he said things straight out, exactly as he saw them. But Chris sees his Asperger syndrome as a good thing – it allows him to see the world in incredible detail and sharpness. He believes it is an important part of who he is.

One of his teachers taught Chris how to preserve and stuff dead animals – a skill called taxidermy.

WILDLIFE WATCH

Chris learned all about kestrels, shrews and badgers as a teenager, and carried on doing so at Southampton University, where he studied zoology – the science of animals and how they live. As well as studying creatures, Chris was a punk rocker, playing in a band called the Titanic Survivors. To Chris, the creative, rule-breaking punk spirit went hand in hand with fighting for human and animal rights.

After he finished studying, Chris wanted to do something more creative, so he began taking photos of wildlife. He took a job as a wildlife cameraman to help pay for the equipment he needed. Soon, though, he was in front of the camera himself, presenting programmes like *The Really Wild Show* on CBBC from 1986 to 1995, which taught children about wildlife in different countries, and *The Great British Birdwatch*. With his own company, Head over Heels, Chris also made shows for the Discovery Channel and National Geographic.

Then, in 2009, he began presenting *Springwatch*, a hugely popular BBC programme which shows the movement and change of wildlife in the spring, as young creatures are born. He also presents the shows *Autumnwatch* and *Winterwatch*.

Chris has travelled all around the world, visiting places from the Everest mountain range to deserts and rainforests, as well as diving deep into the ocean. He's presented shows like *Nature's Weirdest Events* and *World's Sneakiest Animals*, giving his viewers a glimpse into the strangest and most fascinating corners of the animal kingdom – as well as filming things closer to home, like *Cats v. Dogs*!

Since the 1990s, Chris has suffered from Ménière's disease, which affects the inner ear and can make people feel dizzy, as well as affecting their hearing. He has also suffered from depression, especially after losing his dog Fish.

ACTION AGAINST ANIMAL CRUELTY

Chris believes strongly in taking action to stop the abuse of animals and to educate people about it. In 2014, he used his own money to take a film crew to Malta, where they shot footage of migrating and endangered birds being killed in huge numbers by hunters. While filming there, Chris was arrested and held for three hours – but after he was released, his footage helped raise thousands of euros for charities trying to end the hunting of birds.

Chris now lives in the New Forest, still writing, campaigning and presenting nature shows, sometimes even alongside his step-daughter, Megan McCubbin! Although there are enormous challenges facing animal lovers and conservationists today, he believes that we can rise up to meet and overcome them, and that we owe it to the world to do so.

EMMELINE PANKHURST

When Emmeline Pankhurst was born, women in Britain were not allowed to vote. Throughout her life, she fought to win women the same voting rights as men – and just as she died, the results of her long fight finally became law.

RADICAL PARENTS

In July 1858, a baby was born in Manchester to Robert and Sophia Goulden. They both believed strongly in women being allowed to vote, which was unusual at the time. The little girl, Emmeline, was their first child, but she wasn't an only child for very long – over the next few years her parents had nine more children!

   As the eldest daughter, Emmeline had to look after her siblings. It was said she learned to read when she was only three – after that, it was her job to read the newspaper to her father in the mornings too. While doing this, she learned a lot about politics and what was happening in the world. The family lived in a pretty white house called Seedley Cottage, some way outside the busy city centre. Emmeline had a happy childhood here, full of books, plays and games with her brothers and sisters.

> *Emmeline's father enjoyed theatre and acting – at one point he even owned a theatre in Salford! Emmeline learned a lot about the power of drama from him.*

WHY SHOULD GIRLS BE DIFFERENT?

When Emmeline was in bed one night, pretending to be asleep, she heard her father say, "What a pity she wasn't born a lad." Although he thought women should have the vote, he still thought educating his sons was more important than educating his daughters – something that made Emmeline angry, sad and determined to make a change.

When Emmeline was 14, her mother took her to a women's suffrage (the right to vote) meeting. After that, she became inspired by the idea of winning women the vote. Why should boys be taught differently from girls – and why should men and not women be allowed to choose the country's government by voting?

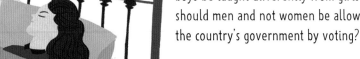

WOMEN'S SUFFRAGE

A year later, Emmeline went away to school in Paris. In 1878, when she came back to Manchester, she met a barrister called Richard Pankhurst, who believed in the same things she did. Although he was more than 20 years older than her, they fell in love, and were married in 1879. Over the next 10 years, they had five children together.

Although she now spent a lot of time looking after her family, Emmeline was determined not to stop working for women's suffrage. In 1889, she and Richard founded the Women's Franchise League (WFL) together. The WFL fought for women's right to vote – but the members found it impossible to agree with each other, and the organisation soon came to an end.

Richard died in 1898, leaving Emmeline a widow. In 1903, two of Emmeline's daughters, Sylvia and Christabel, encouraged their mother to set up a new organisation called the Women's Social and Political Union (WSPU), which aimed to win the vote for women at any cost. As well as speeches and big meetings, the WSPU used aggressive, sometimes violent methods – smashing windows and chaining themselves to railings – to draw attention to them and to stop their demands being ignored.

Emmeline and other WSPU members were often treated cruelly when they were arrested. They were kept in solitary confinement and when they protested by refusing to eat, they were fed by force. Although at first many people thought what they were doing was wrong, when news of their harsh treatment reached the public, support for their cause increased.

> "We are here not because we are law-breakers; we are here in our efforts to become law-makers."

THE RIGHT TO VOTE

Emmeline was arrested multiple times and imprisoned. When she was put on trial for her behaviour, she argued very well for the WSPU's cause in court.

Angered by slow progress and broken promises, in 1913, the WSPU even started committing arson – the crime of setting fire to things. Emmeline's daughters Sylvia and Adela disagreed with these extreme tactics. They quarrelled with their mother and sister Christabel, and broke away from the WSPU.

When the First World War began in 1914, Emmeline and Christabel stopped taking action to demand the vote. Instead, they encouraged everyone to join the war effort. They even handed white feathers to men they thought should be in the army, to shame them into joining – something many people later thought was wrong. During the war, women took over many jobs that had only been done by men before, and this helped to change more people's views on their strength and intelligence. In 1918, the vote was given to some groups of women over 30, like those who owned or lived in a certain kind of house or property.

Emmeline's health was now poor and it got worse as she grew older. In 1928, all women aged 21 and over were finally given the right to vote. Shortly before this officially became law, the woman who had fought so hard and long to win that right died. A statue of her stands by the Palace of Westminster.

> "Women are very slow to rouse, but once they are aroused, once they are determined, nothing on earth and nothing in heaven will make women give way; it is impossible."

BEATRIX POTTER

If you've ever read or watched *The Tale of Peter Rabbit*, you've enjoyed Beatrix Potter's work. Her dainty little books about smartly dressed, sometimes naughty animals have sold more than 150 million copies around the world – even though, at first, no one wanted to publish them!

A CITY CHILDHOOD

On 28th July 1866, a little girl called Helen Beatrix Potter was born to wealthy parents in the smart London neighbourhood of Kensington. Like most girls at the time, Beatrix was never sent to school. Instead, she was kept at home and taught by governesses.

Alone in the nursery at the top of the house, clever, artistic Beatrix often felt frustrated, though she loved reading fairy tales, and drawing her own versions of "Cinderella" and "Sleeping Beauty". She also loved summer holidays in Scotland, and later the Lake District, far away from their dark London house – the lush green Lake District was where she felt truly at home.

Since they had few human friends to play with, Beatrix and her younger brother, Walter Bertram, kept a whole zoo of pets: several mice, a hedgehog, bats, insects, frogs and rabbits. Her parents, who loved nature and art, encouraged their children to sketch their animal companions, and Beatrix used a microscope to look at tiny creatures and draw them. She also wrote stories about her pets' adventures.

> As a teenager, Beatrix began writing a journal in a secret code. It was filled with her thoughts about art, her daily life and her pets. The code wasn't cracked until 1952, when a Potter superfan called Leslie Linder discovered how to translate it. It took him nine years!

When she grew up, Beatrix's parents expected her either to marry someone rich or to help run the household. But Beatrix was more interested in learning about animals and the rest of the natural world. She even wrote a paper about fungi spores which was presented by a male scientist to a famous natural history organisation called the Linnaean Society, because women weren't allowed in.

She still loved pets as a grown-up. One of her favourites was Benjamin Bouncer, a "very tame and clever" Belgian rabbit. In the 1890s, Beatrix began making Benjamin Bouncer greetings cards, which sold very well, to Beatrix's delight. At last, she might be able to make her own money and spend it how she liked!

FOUR LITTLE RABBITS

In 1893, she wrote a letter to Noel, the son of her old governess, who was ill. To cheer him up, she told him a story about four little rabbits, "whose names were Flopsy, Mopsy, Cottontail, and Peter", and illustrated it with her own drawings. Noel's mother suggested that Beatrix should try to publish the story.

At first, all the publishers Beatrix approached said no. She wanted her books to be small and easy for children to hold, and the publishers thought they should be bigger and more expensive. So Beatrix paid for 250 copies of *The Tale of Peter Rabbit* to be privately printed. They sold so fast that Frederick Warne & Co then agreed to publish *The Tale of Peter Rabbit* in 1902 – it sold over 50,000 copies in just one year!

Beatrix quickly became an incredibly successful author, following Peter Rabbit with stories of Squirrel Nutkin, Benjamin Bunny, Mrs Tiggy-Winkle the hedgehog, and Jemima Puddle-Duck. Her little books, with their delicate, realistic pictures and mischievous creatures, are still loved today by children all over the world.

Beatrix was a clever businesswoman. In 1903 she designed a Peter Rabbit doll – this was followed by a Peter Rabbit board game, china tea sets and other toys, all of which made a lot of money for Beatrix and her publishers.

A LOVE OF THE LAND

With the money Beatrix earned from her stories, she was able to buy a farm in Near Sawrey, a part of the Lake District she had always loved. She carried on buying land there for many years. When William Heelis, a local solicitor and close friend of Beatrix's, proposed to her in 1912, her parents disapproved, but they couldn't stop her marrying him.

Beatrix – now Mrs Heelis – flung herself into farming life. Dressed in clogs and heavy tweed clothes, she looked after her farms and flocks of Herdwick sheep, which often won prizes at shows. She stopped painting when her eyesight became weak, although she continued to sketch for the rest of her life. Beatrix had little time for fans peering over her garden wall, expecting her to be as dainty as her books. But when she died, in 1943, she left 15 farms and 4,000 acres of land to the National Trust, to be preserved for everyone to enjoy as much as she and Peter Rabbit had.

MARY PRINCE

Though Mary Prince was enslaved for most of her life, and often treated cruelly, she became a powerful voice for the rights of enslaved people. One of the first Black female authors to publish an autobiography, she helped show how much suffering slavery caused.

ENSLAVED FROM BIRTH

Mary Prince was born in Bermuda, at a farm called Brackish Pond, in 1788. Her father and mother were both enslaved people. This meant Mary was enslaved too, from the moment she was born, and treated as though she did not have the right to be paid for her work or to choose where she lived or what she did. Mary's mother 'belonged' to an enslaver called Charles Myners, which meant that Mary was considered to be his property too. He died when Mary was still a baby, and she and her family were given to a sailor, Captain Williams.

Captain Williams was a harsh man with a bad temper, and Mary dreaded the times when he was home from the sea. His wife and daughter were kinder to her, though. When she was hired out to work for a woman called Mrs Pruden, her daughter, Fanny, began teaching Mary to read. Mary enjoyed learning her letters and how to spell short words.

But when Mrs Williams died, more tragedy struck for Mary and her sisters. They were separated and each sold to a different enslaver, never to see each other again.

"All that we love taken away from us – Oh, it is sad, sad! and sore to be borne!"

A HARD LIFE

Mary now found herself in the household of Captain John Ingham. Both he and his wife were cruel and wicked people. They beat and punished the enslaved people in their home, forcing them to work from early in the morning until well into the night, milking cows, tending children, cooking food and growing crops. When an old jug that was already cracked broke in Mary's hands, her enslavers beat her until she couldn't stand up. Mary was happy to be sent away by ship to another island and another enslaver – but there she was made to work in the salt fields, where salt was collected to be sold. She had to stand in salt water for hours every day, which made painful boils rise on her skin. All the workers here were treated even more badly, and their pain distressed her almost as much as her own.

TRYING TO BE FREED

After many years of work in the salt fields and in Bermuda, Mary asked if she could be sold to a man called John Wood, who was going to Antigua, hoping that she would have an easier and more pleasant life there. But John Wood and his wife were also harsh and demanding. When Mary's body ached and swelled all over with an illness called rheumatism, they still insisted she wash enormous tubs of clothes, and beat her if she didn't satisfy them.

Mary now joined the Moravian Church, where she finally learned to read. Here, she met a carpenter called Daniel James, who had also been enslaved, but had bought his freedom by giving his enslaver money. Daniel and Mary fell in love and agreed to marry in 1826 – much to the fury of Mr and Mrs Wood, who beat her again for daring to choose a husband. By now, Mary had earned and saved enough money to buy her own freedom, but the Woods refused to let her go, or to allow anyone else to buy her.

> *"I have been a slave—I have felt what a slave feels, and I know what a slave knows; and I would have all the good people in England to know it too, that they may break our chains, and set us free."*

SHARING HER STORY

The Woods sailed to England in 1828, taking Mary with them. She asked to go, hoping that she could be cured of her rheumatism there. However, their unreasonable demands continued. Although Mary had a little more independence in England under British law, she didn't know anyone there, so she couldn't earn a living when the Woods threatened to throw her out. She couldn't go back to Antigua and her husband, either, without becoming enslaved again. She eventually fled to the Moravian Church in London, and found work with Thomas Pringle, the Secretary of the Anti-Slavery Society, an organisation which was working to help set all enslaved people free. Thomas suggested that Mary should tell her own story, in her own words, to a woman called Susanna Strickland, who would write it down.

> *In 1829, Mary became the first Black woman ever to present a petition to the British government, arguing for enslaved people's right to freedom.*

THE FIGHT TO ABOLISH SLAVERY

Two years later, in 1831, Mary's autobiography, *The History of Mary Prince, A West Indian Slave,* was published. Her clear, direct way of telling her story, and the horror and pain of the experiences she described, had a big impact on the people who read her book – in one year, it sold out three printings. Like Olaudah Equiano (page 42), Mary Prince was a vital part of the movement to abolish slavery – her story showed how wrong it was to take away freedom from human beings, to treat them badly, and to tear them away from the people they loved.

Not much is known about Mary's life after this. She may have died around 1833, the year the Slavery Abolition Act was passed, banning slavery. However, if she was still alive, she may have returned to Antigua as a free woman, to be reunited with her husband at last.

The History of Mary Prince
A West Indian Slave

ANITA RODDICK

Born into a hardworking Italian family, Anita Roddick took one tiny little shop in Brighton and turned it into the huge Body Shop chain, sticking to her strong environmental values all the way! She changed the way many people thought about what they bought and how they did business.

A DRAMATIC ARRIVAL

In 1942, in the middle of the Second World War, Anita Perilli was born in a strange place – a bomb shelter in Littlehampton, Sussex! She was the third of four children in her Italian family – there were very few immigrant families where she lived, which made her even more unusual. But Anita's life would more than live up to her extraordinary beginnings.

Anita's mother, Gilda, ran the family café – careful and resourceful, she recycled as much as she could, and taught her children to do the same. Anita worked there from a young age, carrying trays and running the coffee machine, and learning a lot about hard work and running a business. She often had to get up before dawn to make breakfast for local fishermen! Despite the early hours and tiring work, Anita always looked up to her bold, brave mother: "Everything I am I can lay at the feet of Gilda, the woman who went hot-air-ballooning in her eighties."

When she left school, Anita first wanted to become an actor and then she trained as a teacher, but found that wasn't her passion. Instead, she worked in France and Switzerland, and then went travelling all around the world. She journeyed through Australia, Africa and Asia, learning about how people lived in other countries and also about the products they used to care for their bodies.

When she came home to England, she fell in love with a man called Gordon Roddick, who was just as adventurous and wild as she was herself. She got married to him in 1970, and they began running a small restaurant together. Six years later, when they had two daughters, Gordon set off on a journey he'd wanted to make all his life – a horseback ride from Buenos Aires in Argentina, all the way to New York City in the USA! Anita thought this crazy idea was brilliant. She sent him off cheerfully, knowing she wouldn't see him for another two years.

CAFE

BREAKFAST

THE BODY SHOP

But while Gordon was away, Anita needed to earn money for herself and her daughters – so, with a £4,000 loan from the bank, she opened the first Body Shop in Brighton in 1976. Wedged between two funeral homes, it wasn't the best place for a shop selling beauty products! The walls were so damp that she painted them dark green to disguise the mould – the colour that later became the Body Shop's hallmark – but she made sure that it was welcoming to customers, and smelled lovely.

It was important to Anita that her soaps and lotions were environmentally friendly in every way possible. At the time, almost everyone making products like Anita's tested them on animals to be sure they were safe for humans to use. Anita utterly refused to use animal testing, which was a revolutionary decision. She also insisted that the people who supplied ingredients for the products must be paid fairly, and she asked her customers to bring containers back to be refilled – partly to save resources, and partly because they were short of bottles!

Anita never allowed anyone to tell her she couldn't make a difference. As she said herself: "If you think you're too small to have an impact, try going to bed with a mosquito."

PRINCIPLES BEFORE PROFITS

The long hours in her mother's café had prepared her for the hard work of running a shop. The Body Shop was such a success that Anita soon opened another. When Gordon came home, he suggested letting other people open branches of The Body Shop in other places – something called 'franchising' – and the business took off.

Anita never wanted to be a huge business success – not if that meant mistreating the environment, or her workers, suppliers or customers. She certainly didn't expect her shop to become a chain that would be known and loved around the world. But by 1990, Anita was the fourth-richest woman in Britain. In 2003, when she stepped down from running The Body Shop, it had almost 2,000 stores worldwide, selling beauty products to over 77 million customers.

When Anita died in 2007, she was remembered as an activist who gave huge sums of money to counter global warming and to fight injustice, and also as a brilliant businesswoman who always put principles before profits. She changed the way millions of people thought about what they bought.

As well as The Body Shop, Anita helped set up The Big Issue, the magazine sold by homeless people, and founded Children on the Edge, a charity that helps children affected by war and disability. Her own foundation also gave away millions of pounds to organisations like Greenpeace and Women's Aid.

MARY SEACOLE

Born in Jamaica to a Scottish father and Jamaican mother, Mary Seacole travelled the world nursing sick and wounded soldiers, despite the difficulties and prejudice she faced along the way. She even put her "Wonderful Adventures" into a book!

PLAYING NURSE

Mary was born in Kingston, Jamaica, at the beginning of the 19th century. Her father was Captain James Grant, a Scottish army officer, and her mother was a healer or 'doctress', who practised traditional Jamaican medicine. Her mother ran a guest house called Blundell Hall. Here, young Mary played nurse with her poor doll – who caught all the illnesses in Kingston! Her mother taught her how to gather herbs and plants, how to make medicines and how to give them to patients. Even as a little girl, Mary knew she wanted to become a doctress herself.

When Mary was 12, she began helping run her mother's guest house. Many of the people who stayed there were sick or injured British soldiers. Mary had learned enough from her mother by now to help treat their wounds and illnesses.

In 1821, when Mary was a teenager, she travelled to England for the first time with relatives. She loved the excitement of the eight-week voyage and being in London – but she was annoyed when some rude children made comments about the colour of her Black friend's skin. Mary would travel a lot more in her lifetime – and she would get used to dealing with people who made rude remarks like this, telling them that she hoped they would learn better manners!

> Mary's father died when she was 10, but she remembered the thrilling stories of battles and adventure he told her – and, just like him, she longed to travel the world.

KEEPING CHEERFUL

Back in Jamaica, Mary married an English man, Edwin Horatio Hamilton Seacole, in 1836. They ran a store together in the busy Jamaican port of Black River. Sadly, Edwin's health wasn't good, and despite Mary's careful nursing, he died in 1844. Mary's mother died soon after. Although she was now alone and had to work hard to afford to live, Mary stayed cheerful. By now, she was known as a skilled nurse, so she was never short of patients – and she always took the chance to learn from army doctors when they stayed with her. In 1850, a serious illness called cholera made many people ill in Jamaica, and Mary treated lots of patients successfully with her mother's medicines.

A journalist called *William Howard Russell*, who covered the conflict in *Crimea*, called *Mary* "a warm and successful physician, who doctors and cures all manner of men with extraordinary success. She is always in attendance near the battlefield to aid the wounded and has earned many a poor fellow's blessing."

MOTHER SEACOLE

In 1854, Britain joined the Crimean War, which was being fought between Russia and Turkey. Mary learned that illness was killing many of the soldiers in Crimea – some of them were the British soldiers she had nursed herself when they were stationed in Jamaica. She knew that the British Army needed nurses, so she sailed to London to volunteer.

But when she offered her services, the War Office refused her, despite the fact she was an experienced nurse. They said that she had applied too late – or perhaps it was because Mary was a woman of colour. Although Florence Nightingale (page 74) had been able to get support from the British government to hire a team of nurses and set up a battlefield hospital, Mary was given no help at all. However, she did not give up. Teaming up with a friend called Thomas Day, Mary used her own money to travel to Crimea and set up a lodging house called the British Hotel, providing "comfortable quarters for sick and convalescent officers".

While she was in Crimea, Mary sold food and drink to soldiers, and treated their illnesses and injuries at her Hotel. She often rode to the battlefield on her horse with medicines and bandages too. Once, she had to dive off her horse to avoid gunfire and dislocated her thumb! Her kindness to the soldiers she nursed led them to call her "Mother Seacole".

When she arrived back in Britain in 1856, after the troops had left Crimea, Mary had used up all her money and had nothing left to live on. Many grateful soldiers tried to raise money for her by putting on a special concert, but unfortunately it didn't raise as much money as they had hoped. Mary continued to work as a doctress until the end of her life.

Mary died in 1881. For a long time after her death her achievements were forgotten, but in the 21st century, they were celebrated again. In 2004, Mary was voted the greatest Black Briton. A statue of her was put up outside St Thomas' Hospital in London in 2016 – the first statue to honour a Black woman in the United Kingdom.

In *1857*, her autobiography *Wonderful Adventures of Mrs Seacole in Many Lands* was published – one of the first known autobiographies by a writer of colour, and the first by a free woman of colour in the *British Empire*.

ERNEST SHACKLETON

A farmer's son who went to sea, Ernest Shackleton would later become a world-famous polar explorer, pushing the limits of human endurance and inspiring many others who came after him.

DREAMING OF THE SEA

Ernest Shackleton was born in County Kildare, Ireland, in 1874, the second of 10 children – two sons and eight daughters! His father owned a farm near the city of Dublin, and Ernest loved running wild there. Mischievous and lively, he liked to play tricks on his sisters, but his charm usually kept him out of trouble. When Ernest was six, his father decided to study medicine in Dublin, and moved his family to the city. Four years later, they moved again – this time away from Ireland altogether, to the busy suburbs of London.

Young Ernest was taught at home by a governess at first, and then later sent to school. He loved to read, especially books about sailing and the sea, but he didn't try very hard at his lessons, and often annoyed his teachers by strolling in late. He didn't like studying poetry, although he enjoyed reading it and dreaming of faraway places. And even though he would grow up to be one of the world's most famous explorers, he didn't learn much geography! His father wanted him to be a doctor, just like him. But Ernest wanted to follow a different path.

At age 16, he left school – surprising his teachers by passing his exams with excellent marks – and joined the merchant navy as a sailor aboard the *Hoghton Tower*. This ship was bound for Chile, which meant sailing round a headland called Cape Horn on the southern tip of South America – famously stormy and difficult to navigate! Ernest had to learn an awful lot very quickly on his first voyage. But he loved the challenges and the companionship of being on a ship, and realised that the roving life of a sailor was indeed the one he wanted.

Ernest saw exploration and adventure as part of being human. As he wrote himself: "I believe it is in our nature to explore, to reach out into the unknown. The only true failure would be not to explore at all."

VOYAGE TO THE POLE

In 1898, Ernest became a Master Mariner, meaning he could now command any ship. Not long after, he was introduced to Sir Clements Markham, who was in charge of the British National Antarctic Expedition, and given the position of third officer on the research steamship *Discovery*. With Robert Falcon Scott in charge, the goal of this expedition was to be the first in the world to reach the South Pole. Ernest hoped that the voyage would make him famous. He had been in love with a woman called Emily Dorman for years, and he wanted to impress Emily so that she would agree to marry him.

The *Discovery* set out in July 1901, with a full crew (and 25 Siberian sled dogs) on board. After half a year of sailing, the ship arrived at the Antarctic coast. The crew began gathering information about the weather and wildlife of this icy place and some of them set out across the ice to try and reach the Pole. But the quality of their food was so bad that most of them, including Ernest, suffered from a disease called scurvy. They were too weak to complete their trek and they had to turn back. Ernest was so ill that he had to be sent home. (Despite this, Emily was impressed – she and Ernest got married in 1904!)

In 1908, Ernest set out on another expedition, this time leading it himself. He got even closer to the Pole and made important scientific discoveries. When he returned, he was made a knight – Sir Ernest Shackleton.

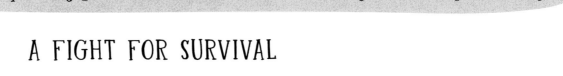

When Ernest advertised for men to join the *Endurance* expedition, nearly 5,000 applied. He chose his party by asking questions about their skills – including whether they could sing!

A FIGHT FOR SURVIVAL

But in 1911, Ernest's hopes of being the first person in the world to reach the South Pole were dashed – the Norwegian explorer Roald Amundsen successfully made the trip. (Robert Falcon Scott was not far behind him, but he died of starvation before he could return to England.) Ernest was still fascinated by polar exploration, though. In 1914, he returned to the Antarctic with the *Endurance*, intending to cross the whole continent via the Pole – the first time this had ever been done.

But when the expedition reached Antarctica, the *Endurance* became trapped in the ice, and was eventually crushed and destroyed in November 1915. When the ship sank, the expedition's chance of crossing the continent vanished too. Ernest and his crew now had to work desperately hard just to stay alive, camping on the ice floes for months. In April 1916, they took to the sea again in small boats and made their way to the tiny Elephant Island. From here, Ernest and five of his crew sailed in a lifeboat across freezing, terrifying seas to South Georgia, where they were able to get help for the others. Although the expedition failed to cross Antarctica, all of the stranded crew survived.

Ernest died of a heart attack in 1922 at the age of 47 during a fourth expedition, hoping to sail all round Antarctica. He was buried on South Georgia. Though he never managed to reach the South Pole, his courage inspired many others to continue exploring, setting out to discover the most mysterious regions of the Earth.

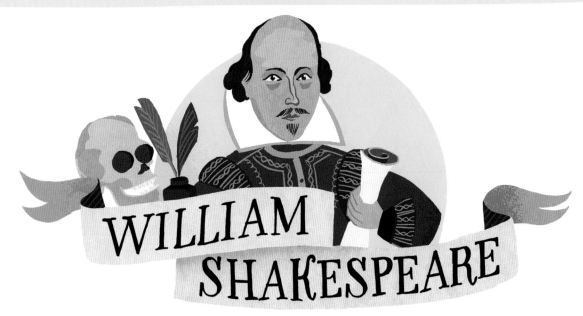

WILLIAM SHAKESPEARE

Have you ever heard someone say "in a pickle", "a sorry sight", or "set my teeth on edge"? All these phrases were invented by the playwright William Shakespeare – as well as words like 'arch-villain', 'addiction' and 'ladybird'! Although he wrote his plays more than 400 years ago, we still use his language every day.

YOUNG SHAKESPEARE

We don't know a lot about William Shakespeare's early life, because it was so long ago. No one knew how important this little boy would turn out to be, so they didn't write down lots of facts about his childhood. We do know he was baptised on 26th April 1564, in the town of Stratford-upon-Avon. His birthday is celebrated on 23rd April (although no one knows exactly when it was). William's parents lived comfortably, although they weren't rich or high-born. His father, John, made fine leather gloves, and his mother, Mary Arden, was the daughter of a wealthy farmer.

William was the oldest child in his family, and had three brothers and two sisters (most people at that time had large families, as children often died very young). He almost certainly went to the grammar school in Stratford, where he would have learned a lot of Latin and perhaps acted in Latin plays too. He might also have gone to see travelling actors performing plays when they came to Stratford. In 1582, soon after he left school, 18-year-old William married a farmer's daughter called Anne Hathaway. Their daughter Susanna was born not long afterwards. Boy and girl twins, Hamnet and Judith, followed two years later.

After this, no one knows what William got up to until 1592. By then, he was in London, and had already become an actor and a playwright. He seems to have lived mostly there after that, close to the playhouses, but away from Anne and his children in Stratford. Another writer called Robert Greene wrote that he was an "upstart Crow", calling him proud and boastful, and a thief of other people's ideas!

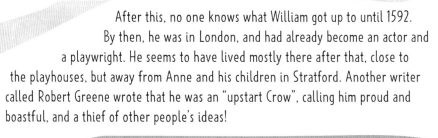

Many people have suggested what William might have got up to during the mysterious 'lost years' of 1585 to 1592 – including being exiled for deer-stealing – but no one knows for sure.

POPULAR PLAYS

William actually spelled his surname "Shakspere", although Shaxper, Shackspeare and Shakespear have all been used too!

Between about 1589 and 1613, William wrote at least 37 plays, as well as 154 sonnets and two long poems. He wrote everything: tragedies (which end in death), comedies (which end in marriage) and histories, which retell events that really happened and are usually to do with the kings and queens who ruled at the time. And he *did* steal ideas from other stories – most of his plots weren't made up, but taken from tales or songs that already existed. But what he did with these stories was tell them in such powerful language – rich poetry, or rude, funny prose – that his versions became the most popular.

Some of his most famous plays are tragedies – like *Romeo and Juliet*, the sad story of two young lovers from warring families, *Hamlet*, in which a king's son avenges his father's murder, and *Macbeth*, who is a Scottish nobleman who commits crime after crime to become king.

William had to be very careful with his history plays, as they were often performed for Queen Elizabeth I (page 40), or for King James I (VI in Scotland), who ruled after her. In *Richard III*, for example, William made King Richard an evil man because Elizabeth's grandfather, Henry Tudor, had taken the throne from him. If he had shown Richard as a kind, unjustly defeated king, it would have dangerously offended the queen!

BARD OF AVON

In William's own time, his work was successful – enough that he was able to buy a big house in Stratford in 1597! However, people didn't think he was a better playwright than Christopher Marlowe or Ben Jonson, who aren't so well known now. In fact, lots of people thought more of his poems than his plays. His history plays were the most popular, perhaps because the idea of who would rule the country next worried a lot of people, especially as Queen Elizabeth I grew older.

It wasn't till almost 100 years after his death that people began to value him so highly, or to think of his tragedies, like *Hamlet* and *King Lear*, as his greatest work. Now his plays are performed and studied in countries all round the world and translated into almost every language. He is called the English national poet, the 'Bard of Avon' and maybe even the most important playwright of all time. There's even a special word for Shakespeare-worship: 'bardolatry'!

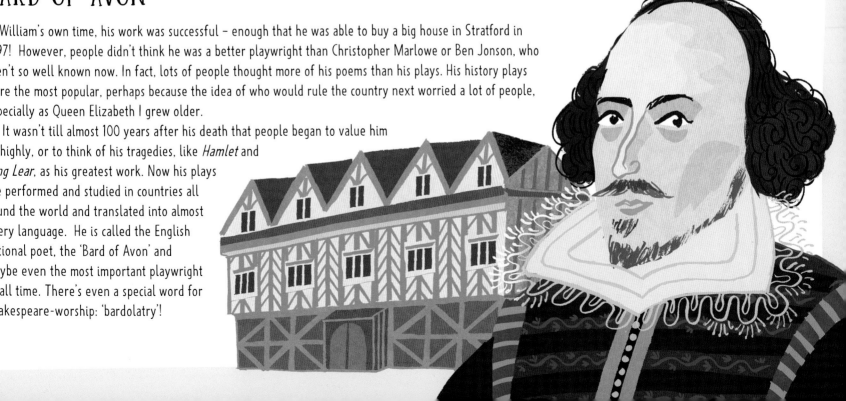

HELEN SHARMAN

From a quiet little house in Sheffield to a space station floating in orbit, the scientist Helen Sharman has travelled further than most other human beings – in 1991, she became the first British person to go into space!

CHOOSING SCIENCE

Helen Sharman was born in 1963 in Sheffield. Her mother was a nurse and her father taught at a college. The family lived in a comfortable house in the suburbs – Mum, Dad, Helen, her sister, Andrea, and brother, James. Helen was a cheerful little girl, who wanted to be a nurse like her mother, or perhaps a ballet dancer. She was very down-to-earth – Andrea liked dressing up, but Helen preferred practical clothes like trousers, and she almost never got upset or angry. She enjoyed music, learning to play the piano, saxophone and recorder, and she liked working hard and discovering new things.

When Helen was 16 and deciding what to study next, one of her teachers told her that if she picked physics and chemistry, she'd be the only girl in those classes. But Helen didn't let that stop her – she went ahead and studied science. She was also good at learning other languages, which would come in very handy one day. After school and university, she moved to London, where she studied for a PhD in chemistry, and then worked as an engineer.

Even as a child, Helen never had a problem with heights. She liked to climb to the top of a tall tree and read a book to relax, and she enjoyed fairground rides – the scarier the better!

ASTRONAUT WANTED

Helen's next job was a delicious one. She became a chemist with Mars Confectionery, working on the chemistry of chocolate and ice cream! But while this might have seemed like a dream job, Helen had further to go. Driving home from work one day in 1989, she heard an exciting job advert on the radio: "Astronaut wanted – no experience necessary". Her first thought was that she wouldn't be chosen – then she realised she definitely wouldn't be if she didn't even try! So she applied – and got the job. Her scientific training, fitness and her knowledge of other languages helped her to come first out of more than 13,000 applicants.

Project Juno was a joint mission between Britain and the Soviet Union, intended to take three astronauts into space. Helen left for Russia almost straight away. Here, she learned to speak Russian and was trained to cope with strong G-forces and zero gravity. It was 18 months before she and the two Soviet astronauts on the mission were finally ready for launch.

Helen was always a fearless traveller. When she was at university, she worried her mother by getting a motorbike – and repairing it herself!

FIRST BRITON IN SPACE

Then the day arrived. In May 1991, Helen Sharman became the first Briton in space. She took off from the place now called Kazakhstan in a spacecraft called Soyuz TM-12, burst up through the atmosphere, and spent eight days orbiting the Earth. She spent most of those days on the Mir space station, where she ran experiments and talked to schoolchildren back in Britain over the radio. She also took some seeds into space, to compare with seeds growing on Earth.

"There's no greater beauty than looking at the Earth from up high," Helen said about spaceflight. She wondered at the beauty of the deep blue oceans, the millions and millions of stars, how small the Earth looked – and how huge the universe.

A scientist all her life, Helen now works at Imperial College London. She still dreams of spaceflight – she'd like to go to Mars one day! – and she hopes that there'll be more British astronauts.

Helen believes that aliens must exist, because the universe is so huge and contains so many billions of stars. "It's possible they're here right now and we simply can't see them"!

MARY SHELLEY

The brilliant and rebellious writer Mary Shelley ran away from home when she fell in love with a poet, and became famous around the world for creating a strange, terrifying story of artificial life.

DAUGHTER OF THE FIRST FEMINIST

In 1792, a powerful writer called Mary Wollstonecraft published a book calling for women to have the same rights and education as men. Although it's now seen as the first feminist work, which began the fight for gender equality, back then the ideas in the book were considered shocking. Mary was married to another writer named William Godwin, and on 30th August 1797, she gave birth to a baby girl. Sadly, Mary died only a few days later, so her daughter – also called Mary – would never know her bold, brilliant mother except through her writing.

Little Mary grew up with her older half-sister, Fanny. Reading greedily from her father's huge collection of books, and talking to exciting, intelligent guests like the poets Samuel Taylor Coleridge and William Wordsworth, who were often invited round to dinner, Mary was an imaginative, thoughtful, strong-willed girl, who loved writing her own stories. Though she often thought about the mother she had never known, she was happy at home until her father married again. Mary Jane Clairmont, his new wife, brought her own two children to live with the Godwins, and later had a son with William. But Mary and her stepmother did not get on well. Mary was eventually sent to Scotland to stay with William Baxter, a friend of her father's, and his family.

In one of his letters, her father described the teenage Mary as "singularly bold, somewhat imperious, and active of mind"!

FRANKENSTEIN IS BORN!

When Mary was 16, she fell deeply in love with the poet Percy Bysshe Shelley, who already had a wife, and ran away with him to Italy. Running away, or 'eloping', like this was terribly scandalous – many of the people they knew refused to talk to them. They were often very poor, travelling around Europe in search of places to stay where they would not be looked down on. After Percy's first wife died, Mary married him.

One stormy night in Switzerland in 1816, Mary, Percy and another famous poet, Lord Byron, decided to have a ghost story writing competition. Percy gave up quickly and Byron wrote only a fragment, but Mary's story grew and grew into a novel – a novel that would be published in 1818 as *Frankenstein*. It is the strange, haunting story of a young man, Victor Frankenstein, who gives life to a being he creates and then becomes terrified of his own creation. The book was an instant hit and is still popular today.

Frankenstein is thought of as the world's first science fiction story!

Mary and Percy had three children, but only one of them, their son Percy Florence, survived to adulthood.

LIVING ON THROUGH HER WORK

After Percy died in a boating accident in 1822, Mary returned to London. She was now a widow at only 24, with a small son to support. For the rest of her life, she worked as a writer, publishing several other novels and a science fiction story called *The Last Man*. Though her later work wasn't as wildly successful as *Frankenstein*, she made her living as a woman of letters at a time when this was still very unusual. She also edited Percy's poetry and fought passionately for his work to be recognised.

After her son married, Mary lived happily with him and his wife, Jane, until she died of brain cancer at the age of 53. However, her wild, mysterious, powerful writing would live on for hundreds of years after her death.

After her husband's death, Mary kept his preserved heart with her, wrapped in silk, for the rest of her life. It was found inside her desk after her death.

LEMN SISSAY

Though Lemn Sissay's childhood was hard and miserable, and he was let down by the people who should have cared for him, he grew up to become a brilliant writer – a poet whose work has touched and inspired thousands of readers.

FROM PLACE TO PLACE

When Lemn Sissay's mother came to Britain from Ethiopia in 1966, she didn't yet know she was going to have a baby. After her son was born in 1967, near Wigan in the north of England, she found it hard to look after him, so she asked if he could be cared for by foster parents for a little while. But instead of giving her the help she asked for, a social worker took away her baby, renamed him Norman (the social worker's own name) and gave him to a white family to adopt as their own. His mother wrote letter after letter, asking for her son to be returned, but she got no answer.

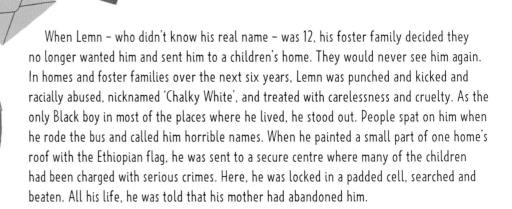

When Lemn – who didn't know his real name – was 12, his foster family decided they no longer wanted him and sent him to a children's home. They would never see him again. In homes and foster families over the next six years, Lemn was punched and kicked and racially abused, nicknamed 'Chalky White', and treated with carelessness and cruelty. As the only Black boy in most of the places where he lived, he stood out. People spat on him when he rode the bus and called him horrible names. When he painted a small part of one home's roof with the Ethiopian flag, he was sent to a secure centre where many of the children had been charged with serious crimes. Here, he was locked in a padded cell, searched and beaten. All his life, he was told that his mother had abandoned him.

> *"I think I'll paint roads on my front room walls to convince myself that I'm going places."*

IMAGINATION IS KEY

Lemn's sad, painful early life hurt him in many ways, but it did not destroy him. He wrote poetry to help himself express his sadness and anger, and to explore much further than his cramped surroundings. He sold his first small collection of poems door-to-door while cleaning people's gutters. When he moved from Wigan to Manchester at the age of 21, his poetry was published in a book for the first time.

SAID THE SUN
TO THE MOON

SAID THE HEAD
TO THE HEART

"WE HAVE MORE IN COMMON

THAN SETS US APART"

LEMN SISSAY

MY NAME IS WHY

After that, he wrote many poetry collections, stage plays and a memoir called *My Name is Why* ('Lemn' means 'why' in Amharic, the main language of Ethiopia). He performed his poetry on stages across the world, presenting the first National Poetry Slam in 2004.

Although Lemn found his birth family eventually, the years they had spent apart meant that it was now just too hard for him to form close bonds with them. But for the first time, Lemn began to see that he was loved. People were deeply moved by his poetry and performances. They valued his powerful work, and painted lines from it on many buildings in Manchester. Lemn's poems are also carved into buildings across London, like the Royal Festival Hall, and in other places around the world.

> *"I investigated the world through my imagination."*

MORE THAN ONE WAY TO LEARN

In 2010, Lemn was awarded an MBE for services to literature, and he was asked to be the first official poet of the 2012 London Olympics. He even wrote the official poem for the 2015 FA Cup! That same year, he was also made Chancellor of the University of Manchester, a hugely important position – and one that amazed Lemn, since he had never been to university himself. But his appointment proved that there is more than one way to learn, and that people who begin life with nothing can make art that speaks to everyone.

For years, Lemn had wanted an apology from the council that had let him down, and in 2018, he finally got it. Wigan Council sent Lemn the files about his early life, gave him money as compensation, and apologised for the ways in which it had failed him as a child. Although no one can give Lemn back his stolen family and childhood, he is now beloved and celebrated, and his work has given hope and joy to thousands.

PAUL STEPHENSON

Paul Stephenson served in the Royal Air Force before becoming one of Britain's most successful and inspiring civil rights activists, campaigning for Black Britons to be treated equally in all areas of life in Britain.

DIFFERENT FROM OTHER CHILDREN

In 1937, a little boy called Paul was born in Essex in the south-east of England. His father was West African and his mother was British, of mixed heritage.

At the beginning of the Second World War, when he was three, Paul was evacuated to a care home in a village called Great Dunmow in Essex, because his mother was working in the army during the war. Paul was sometimes made to feel like the odd one out because of the colour of his skin. A teacher at his school even cut a lock of his hair to keep because it looked so different from their own. People also stared at his mother when she came to visit, because they'd never seen a Black woman in an army uniform before. But he loved playing with his friends, paddling in streams and hunting for rabbits – even if there were no other children there who looked like him.

Paul's grandmother, Edie Johnson, had been a successful West End theatre actress in the 1920s.

ENGLAND WAS HIS COUNTRY

He went back to London in 1947, but even though there were more Black people in the city, he still didn't always feel welcome. He was the only Black child in his secondary school. People would sometimes call him horrible names as he walked down the street, and some teachers treated him badly at school. Paul felt strongly that he was English and that England was his country – many years later, when he wrote his autobiography, he called it *Memoirs of a Black Englishman*. But he often felt as though he didn't belong, or that other people tried to make him feel that way. Throughout his life, he would fight for the right of Black people to be fully included and valued in Britain.

Because Essex Council had taken good care of him as a child and fostered him during the war, Paul and his wife, Joyce, later fostered eight children alongside their own!

THE BRISTOL BUS BOYCOTT

Paul became an Air Force cadet in 1953, and stayed in the RAF until 1960, finishing his education while he was in the service. He also spent a lot of time working with children, especially in the Scouts. This was something else he would keep on doing all his life.

In 1962, he went to Bristol in the south-west of England, to work with young people in the community. He was the city's first Black social worker. Here, he discovered that although Black and Asian people spent money riding on the buses, the Bristol Omnibus Company refused to hire them as bus drivers or conductors. Alongside the Black drivers who had been refused jobs, Paul organised a boycott of the buses, where people refused to use the buses in protest. Support for the boycott spread through Bristol and then to the rest of the country, with famous sportspeople and politicians speaking out on Paul's side. After a few months, the bus company backed down, and began employing people of colour (but Paul lost his teaching job for being "too controversial"!).

"Every generation has a duty to fight against racism, otherwise it will find its way into our country and into our homes. Addressing this challenge is our duty if we wish to seek a happy and prosperous existence."

WELL-KNOWN ACTIVIST

In 1964, Paul went into a pub called the Bay Horse in Bristol. At this time, it was still legal in the United Kingdom for pub landlords and shopkeepers to refuse to serve Black people. Paul had just bought himself a drink when the manager asked him to leave. When Paul calmly said no, the manager called the police. Paul was arrested and spent several hours in a prison cell before being put on trial. Although the policemen who arrested him – eight of them! – said that he had been violent and tried to fight them, another man who had seen everything backed him up. The judge ruled that Paul had been wrongly accused. This event helped to bring in a new law in the United Kingdom called the Race Relations Act (1965), which made it illegal to refuse to serve someone because of their skin colour.

Paul was now well known as an activist. In 1964, he was invited to go to the United States by a group of people who were trying to stop segregation (the separation of people of different skin colours) there. Paul was surprised to be stared at when he went into the hotel where he was staying. He only discovered afterwards that the hotel had never had a Black guest before.

In London, Paul worked with the famous boxer Muhammad Ali to set up a sports association for Black children in Brixton. Paul wanted them to try new activities that they hadn't been able to do before, like table tennis and pony trekking. Cheekily, Paul even managed to get Muhammad Ali to drop in on a school assembly – for free!

Paul continued to work tirelessly for racial equality and to end discrimination, and as he grew older, he was given wider recognition for his achievements. In 2009, he was given an OBE, and in 2017, he received a Pride of Britain Lifetime Achievement Award. He even has a train named after him!

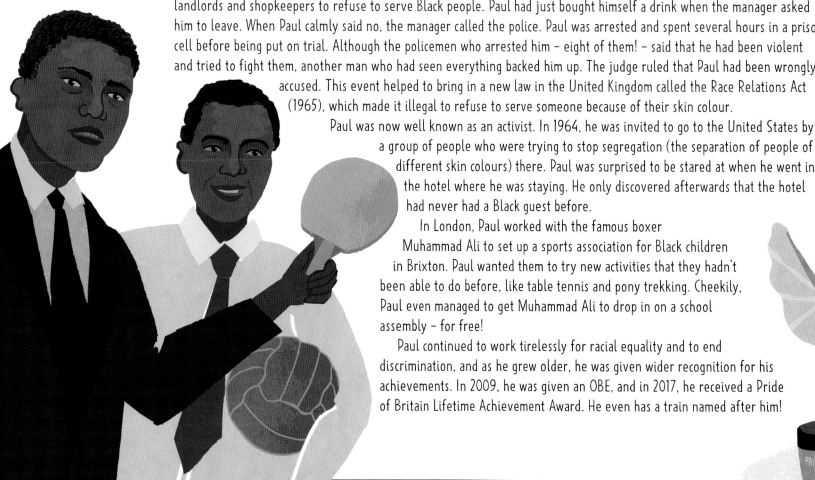

STORMZY

A famous grime artist and performer, Stormzy fights injustice, racism and inequality wherever he finds them, creating chances for people who need them while he tops the charts with his powerful music.

> Apart from Stormzy, Michael has lots of other nicknames, including 'Big Mike', 'The Problem' and 'Wicked Skengman'. 'Big Mike' isn't all that surprising – he's 1.96 metres tall!

NOTHING MORE GANGSTER THAN BEING WELL READ

On a summer day in 1993, a boy called Michael Ebanezer Kwadjo Omari Owuo Jr was born in Croydon, South London. His Ghanaian mum, Abigail, brought him up, taking him to church every week and working three jobs to make sure that Michael, his brother and two sisters always had food to eat. Thornton Heath, their part of Croydon, could be a dangerous place – people often got robbed or hurt – but Michael was happy there, though money was tight at home.

Michael loved school, especially English lessons, where he could write his own poems and stories. He was very competitive and read hundreds of library books to earn prize badges! Although he didn't know it, all that reading was helping develop his gift with words – a gift that would one day make Michael a great rapper and grime artist. As he got older, he was often quite naughty at school, but he still earned several top-grade GCSEs.

> One of Michael's favourite authors as a child was Malorie Blackman (page 18). He mentions her in his song "Superheroes".

But Michael's life wasn't just about school and church. From the age of 11, he went to the local youth club, where he had rap battles with older teenagers. Inspired by the grime music he heard in his neighbourhood, he began to freestyle, improvising his own words over grime beats in his bedroom. Eventually, he started his own YouTube channel, *StormzyTV* – and that's when Michael Omari began to be known better as Stormzy.

ON THE WAY TO THE TOP

When he was 19, bored and miserable, working at an oil refinery, Stormzy decided it was time to try harder to get his music noticed. Although some people thought grime was rude and rough and the sort of music you couldn't play on the radio, he wanted everyone to hear his songs. So he released a collection of tracks called *168: The Mixtape*, and followed it up the next year with a record, *Dreamers Disease*, which won him a MOBO (Music of Black Origin) Award. Then he was invited to perform on the TV show *Later . . . With Jools Holland*. This was the first time an unsigned artist had ever been on the show! Stormzy was on his way to the top.

When his freestyle single "Shut Up" entered the Top 40 in 2015, Stormzy started a campaign to get it to Christmas Number One. It made it to number eight – incredibly impressive for a freestyle track!

SUPERSTAR

In 2017, Stormzy's first full-length album, *Gang Signs & Prayer*, was released, and was an instant UK Number One. Two years later, in 2019, Stormzy became the first Black solo artist to headline Glastonbury, the UK's most famous music festival. Later in 2019, he released his second album, *Heavy Is The Head*. This gave Stormzy his first Number One single, "Vossi Bop".

While playing his Glastonbury set, Stormzy's earpieces broke – he couldn't hear anything, but just had to carry on performing. When he came offstage, he was so afraid that he'd done a terrible job that he cried – much to the surprise of the festival organisers. His show had been a huge success!

NEW OPPORTUNITIES

By now, Stormzy had achieved many amazing things, earned a lot of money and brought the love of grime music to people who had never heard it before. Looking back at his childhood, and realising many talented Black children were missing out on their chances to shine, he decided to use his fame and money to do something about it. He set up a scholarship for Black students to study at the University of Cambridge and started #Merky Books with the publisher Penguin Random House, to publish books and poetry by writers whose voices aren't often heard. In 2020, when people around the world protested against racism, Stormzy pledged to donate £10 million to anti-racist charities.

ALAN TURING

Sometimes called "the father of computer science", Alan Turing was a brilliant thinker whose ideas helped shape the development of computers and artificial intelligence. He's also remembered for his amazing work as a code-breaker during the Second World War.

THINKING DIFFERENTLY

Alan Mathison Turing was born in London in 1912. Throughout his childhood, Alan and his older brother, John, rarely saw their parents – his father was working for the British government in India, so the boys lived with foster parents in the seaside town of Hastings.

It was clear that young Alan was a deep, unusual thinker. As a child, he was particularly inspired by a book called *Natural Wonders Every Child Should Know*, filled with descriptions of how chicks grow and why moths fly towards light. He went to school in Hastings at first, then to a boarding school in Sussex. Some of his teachers were impressed by his intelligence, but others thought he was dreamy and untidy – and things got worse when he started at Sherborne School in Dorset, aged 13.

At Sherborne, his teachers told him off for "slipshod, dirty work", and nearly stopped him taking School Certificate exams (now GCSEs). The headmaster called him "the sort of boy who is bound to be a problem for any school" – not because Alan was naughty or rebellious, but because he thought about things in a different way.

There was a general strike on Alan's first day at Sherborne School, which meant no trains were running. He was so determined to get to school on time that he cycled 63 miles!

But despite this, Alan kept his enthusiasm for science and mathematics. When he was a Sixth Form student, he met Christopher Morcom, another sixth-former who loved science. Christopher was special to Alan – they studied together and both applied to Cambridge University. Then Christopher suddenly died of tuberculosis in 1930. Alan was heartbroken, but felt that he should carry on doing the things Christopher could no longer do. So he accepted a scholarship to study mathematics at King's College, Cambridge.

Here Alan's talent was recognised at last. Aged only 22, he was made a Fellow of the college in 1935, and in 1936 he published a paper called "On Computable Numbers", which laid down the theory of how to program a computer – before computers (as we know them today) even existed.

This impressed everyone, and Alan was invited to study at Princeton University, in the United States.

CODE-BREAKER TO NATIONAL HERO

But across the globe, a terrible conflict was brewing – Germany, under the control of the Nazi Party, was beginning to invade nearby countries, and the world was taking sides. Alan's gift for logic meant he was brilliant at writing and cracking codes. When he returned to Britain in 1938, he was immediately asked to join the Government Code and Cypher School, the organisation in charge of code-breaking and gathering secret information. He went to live and work in their new headquarters at Bletchley Park when war broke out in 1939.

The German military used 'ciphers' to send messages, which were secret codes that their enemies couldn't read. To write messages in code, they used a cipher machine called Enigma. This machine didn't just have one simple cipher – it used wheels to keep changing the letters of the messages, making the codes almost impossible to crack unless you had an Enigma machine yourself. However, in 1941, Alan and his team were finally able to decode the messages from German submarines which had been sinking British ships as they crossed the Atlantic, when Alan invented a powerful code-breaking device called the Bombe. In 1942, he was also the first to crack the complicated codes produced by a German machine called Tunny.

Britain finally won the war in 1945, and Alan's work had played a huge part in that. He was later made an Officer of the Most Excellent Order of the British Empire (OBE). He wasn't just a genius – he was a hero.

Alan couldn't solve every puzzle – including the ones he set himself. In 1940, he converted his savings into silver ingots, and buried them somewhere in Bletchley Park. He returned several times with a map he had drawn, but was never able to find them!

AN EXTRAORDINARY LIFE

After the war, Alan worked on plans for the world's first ever electronic computer, although his design wasn't the one that was finally made. He was also a pioneer in investigating artificial intelligence and developed a test (later called the Turing test) to figure out whether or not a computer was actually thinking. Then he began to look into 'morphogenesis', which is the process of how cells develop. He never stopped thinking about exciting new things to study.

His extraordinary life had a sad, undeserved ending. Alan was gay, which was illegal in Britain until 1967. When police discovered that Alan was in a relationship with a man in 1952, this was considered a crime. As a punishment, he was made to take drugs that were supposed to stop him feeling attracted to men. Two years later, Alan was found dead at his home. Although it's possible that he died accidentally, the official reason recorded was suicide. In 2009, the prime minister Gordon Brown apologised on behalf of the British government for the way in which Alan had been treated, and in 2013 the Queen granted him a royal pardon. We'll never know what other amazing inventions or discoveries he might have made.

MALALA YOUSAFZAI

Resisting attempts to scare her and keep her quiet, including an attack that nearly killed her, the activist Malala Yousafzai has fought fiercely for every girl's right to an education since she was 11 years old.

DEFYING THE TALIBAN

In July 1997, in the city of Mingora in the beautiful, mountainous Swat District of Pakistan, a baby girl was born, the eldest child of Ziauddin and Toor Pekai Yousafzai. Girls in Pakistan were not always valued as highly as boys, but the baby's father, a poet and teacher, believed passionately in education for everyone. He wanted to give his daughter exactly the same opportunities that he would later give his sons.

Young Malala loved school and was a gifted, hard-working student. She shared her father's passion for education, and his belief that it was for everyone.

Ten years after Malala was born, an extremist political group called the Taliban took control of the Swat District. The Taliban believed that girls should not be educated, and that everyone should obey strict religious rules about how they dress and behave. They banned TV, music, make-up, and even flying kites, and harshly punished people who disobeyed. They also began stopping girls from going to school. In 2008, Malala started speaking out against the invaders who had taken away her right to be educated. As the Taliban closed school after school, she wrote down her sad, fearful, angry thoughts, and shared them on a BBC blog. Speaking out in this way was dangerous, but Malala felt that she should tell the world what the Taliban was taking away from the girls of the Swat Valley.

In October 2012, the Taliban tried to silence Malala forever. When she was on her way home from school, an armed man got onto her bus, terrifying the girls, and asked them: "Who is Malala?" He shot her in the head with his gun – but Malala did not die. Ten days later, she woke up in a hospital in Birmingham, UK. Her injuries were very serious, and doctors and nurses had worked desperately to save her life. Offers to help the brave 15-year-old activist had come from hospitals around the world. Malala took a long time to recover, but when she was better, she and her family made a new home in Britain.

> "If one girl with an education can change the world, what can 130 million do?"

THE MALALA FUND

Although Malala considered the UK her second home, she missed the beauty of her mountain valley, and the tastes and smells of the home she had been forced to leave. But she was also determined to seize the chances her new home offered, and to continue fighting for what she believed in. She and her father set up an organisation called the Malala Fund, dedicated to making sure every girl has access to 12 years of free and safe education. The organisation concentrates on the countries where girls are most likely to miss out on going to school as they get older. As well as meeting and helping the girls themselves, they support and train teachers and activists in these places to help their students too. Malala wants to ensure that every girl in the world can choose the future she wants – and have the right education for it.

> "One child, one teacher, one pen and one book can change the world."

NOBEL PEACE PRIZE

In 2013, on her 16th birthday, Malala made a speech to the United Nations, in which she called on the world's leaders to put aside their disagreements, to fight for education and to make sure that women's rights are protected. She also presented a petition to the UN Secretary-General demanding education for all. It had more than 3 million signatures! The day was called 'Malala Day' in her honour.

At age 17, she was given the Nobel Peace Prize – the youngest person ever to receive it. She went on to study at Oxford University, while at the same time continuing to fight injustice for women and girls across the world. In 2020, Malala graduated from university, completing her own education, and one of her hopes for the future is that every other girl should be able to do the same.

> Malala is also a published author!
> Her books include *I Am Malala*,
> the story of her life, and *We Are
> Displaced*, which tells the stories of
> many women throughout the world who
> have had to leave their homes.

GREAT BRITONS TIMELINE

 **BOUDICCA** c.30–c.61

 **ALFRED THE GREAT** 849–899

 **ROBERT THE BRUCE** 1274–1329

 **CHARLOTTE BRONTË** 1816–1855

 **ADA LOVELACE** 1815–1852

 **CHARLES DARWIN** 1809–1882

 **ISAMBARD KINGDOM BRUNEL** 1806–1859

 **FLORENCE NIGHTINGALE** 1820–1910

 **ALEXANDER GRAHAM BELL** 1847–1922

 **EMMELINE PANKHURST** 1858–1928

 **ELSIE INGLIS** 1864–1917

 **SHIRLEY BASSEY** 1937–

 **DAVID ATTENBOROUGH** 1926–

 **JUDITH KERR** 1923–2019

 **YEHUDI MENUHIN** 1916–1999

 **BOBBY CHARLTON** 1937–

 **PAUL STEPHENSON** 1937–

 **IAN McKELLEN** 1939–

 **STEPHEN HAWKING** 1942–2018

 **PAUL McCARTNEY** 1942–

 **MALALA YOUSAFZAI** 1997–

 **STORMZY** 1993–

 **MO FARAH** 1983–

 **KELLY HOLMES** 1970–

106

OWAIN GLYNDŴR

c.1354–c.1416

ELIZABETH I

1533–1603

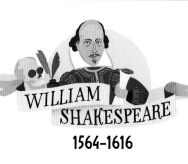

WILLIAM SHAKESPEARE

1564–1616

ISAAC NEWTON

1643–1727

MARY SEACOLE

c.1805–1881

MARY SHELLEY

1797–1851

MARY PRINCE

c.1788–c.1833

WILLIAM BLAKE

1757–1827

OLAUDAH EQUIANO

c.1745–1797

EDITH CAVELL

1865–1915

BEATRIX POTTER

1866–1953

WINSTON CHURCHILL

1874–1965

ERNEST SHACKLETON

1874–1922

ALEXANDER FLEMING

1881–1955

ROALD DAHL

1916–1990

NOOR INAYAT KHAN

1914–1944

ALAN TURING

1912–1954

ANEURIN BEVAN

1897–1960

ANITA RODDICK

1942–2007

FREDDIE MERCURY

1946–1991

TIM BERNERS-LEE

1955–

CHRIS PACKHAM

1961–

TANNI GREY-THOMPSON

1969–

LEMN SISSAY

1967–

HELEN SHARMAN

1963–

MALORIE BLACKMAN

1962–

107

GLOSSARY

activist A person who campaigns publicly or works for an organisation to bring about social or political change.

adoption The act of taking another person's child into your family and him or her legally becoming your own child.

Anglo-Saxons The people who lived in England from the 5th century until the Norman Conquest in 1066.

apprentice Someone who works for a skilled person, such as an engineer or watchmaker, in order to learn their trade.

artificial intelligence A type of technology that makes computers work in a way similar to how human minds work, including making decisions, translating languages and recognising speech.

bacteria Tiny organisms, some of which cause disease.

boarding school A school where pupils live in – sleeping and eating all meals there – during the school term.

cabinet A group of the most senior, or important, ministers in a government who meet to decide its policies.

CERN European Organization for Nuclear Research (the initials stand for French Conseil Européen pour la Recherche Nucléaire), an organisation of European states which does research into high-energy particle physics, based at a centre in Geneva, Switzerland.

civil war A war between different groups of people living in the same country.

clergyman A priest or a vicar in charge of a church and its local area.

colony A country or area that is controlled by another country.

concentration camp A place where large numbers of prisoners are held and forced to work, without enough space, food or medical care, and are sometimes murdered.

conservation An effort to protect and preserve something that is valuable, especially the natural environment.

court A law court is a place where legal matters are decided; a royal court is the place where a king or queen lives and carries out their duties.

Crimean War (1853–1856) Fought between Russia and Great Britain, France and Turkey, mainly around the Black Sea and what is now the Ukraine, over control of land, as well as religious disagreements.

Dame A title given to a woman in recognition of important work she has done or for service to her country.

depression A mental state in which the sufferer feels very sad and unable to enjoy life.

documentary A television or radio programme or a film that gives factual information about a particular subject.

dyslexic A dyslexic person has a learning difference called dyslexia, which affects reading and writing skills.

empire A number of individual nations that are controlled by the government or ruler of a single country.

entrepreneur A person who starts a business.

evolution A process during which plants or animals gradually change some of their physical characteristics over many generations.

feminist A person who believes that men and women are equal and that women should therefore have the same power, rights and opportunities as men.

First World War (1914–1918) The war fought between the Central Powers (led by Germany) and the Allied Powers (led by Great Britain, France, Russia and the USA) over control of Europe, with the Allied Powers winning. Over 16 million people died.

foster family When a child lives with a foster family, he or she becomes part of the family for a period of time without legally becoming the child of their foster parents.

g-force The measurement used to describe the force that the Earth's gravitational field exerts on a body. Astronauts experience high g-forces at take-off and zero gravity when orbiting the Earth.

general strike A situation where most or all of the workers in a country are on strike – refusing to work in an attempt to get better pay or conditions.

grime A type of music that combines elements of garage, hip-hop, rap and jungle.

hygiene The practice of keeping oneself and one's surroundings clean to prevent the spread of disease.

immigrant A person who comes from one country to live in another.

independence People who seek independence for their country wish to have their own government and not be ruled by another country.

Industrial Revolution (Approximately 1760–1840) The process of change from a more traditional society based on farming to a more modern one based on the use of machines, which began in Great Britain.

knight A man may be made a knight in recognition of important work he has done or for service to his country, and he can then use the title Sir.

Latin The language of ancient Rome and until more recent times the language of academic learning as well as church, government and legal documents.

LGBT+   Lesbian, gay, bisexual, transgender plus any other sexual and gender identities.

medieval   Relating to the Middle Ages.

Middle Ages   The period of history between the end of the Roman Empire in 476 and 1500.

monastery   A religious community of monks; the place where they live and worship.

moor   An area of high, open land usually covered with grass and heather.

National Trust   An organisation dedicated to the preservation of historic buildings and areas of natural beauty.

Nazi   A member of the National Socialist German Workers' Party, a harsh and aggressive political movement led by the dictator Adolf Hitler, which controlled Germany from 1933 to 1945.

Nobel Prize   One of six awards given each year to people who have done important work in science, literature, economics, or for world peace.

Olympic Games   An important international sports festival held every four years, each time in a different country. Events include athletics, football, swimming and gymnastics.

pacifist   A person who is against war and violence.

Paralympic Games   An important international sports festival for athletes with disabilities, held every four years with the Olympic Games.

parliament   The group of people who make decisions for a country and make or change its laws; the building in which these people meet and work.

petition   A document signed by lots of people to ask a government or other organisation to do, or not do, a particular thing.

physics   The scientific study of forces such as light, sound, heat, pressure, gravity and electricity and the way in which they affect objects.

plantation   A large area of land, often in a tropical country, where crops such as tea, rubber, sugar or cocoa are grown.

prejudice   Dislike or unfair treatment of a person or group of people – often of a particular race or religion – without cause or reason.

programming   The process of writing a computer program – a series of coded instructions needed for a computer to perform a task.

racism   prejudice or discrimination against someone of a different skin colour or physical appearance; the belief that one's own race is superior to another.

Red Cross   An international organisation that helps people who are suffering as a result of war or natural disasters.

refugee   Someone who has been forced to leave their home or country to escape a natural disaster, war or persecution.

revolution   When a large group of people overthrow the existing government or monarchy of a country by force and install a new system of government.

rights   Things that every member of society is morally allowed to have, such as freedom and equality.

Second World War   (1939–1945) The war fought between the Axis Powers (Germany, Italy and Japan) and the Allied Powers (France, Great Britain, the USA and Russia), partly in continuation of the problems of the First World War. The Allies eventually won the war. Around 50 million people were killed.

social worker   A person whose job is to give help and advice to people who are suffering from serious family or financial problems.

software   Computer programs and operating information.

statistics   The practice or science of collecting and analysing large numbers of facts and figures.

Sufi   A member of a very dedicated and spiritual group of Muslims who seek divine love and knowledge through direct personal experience of Allah (God).

torture   The practice of causing a person great pain in order to punish them or force them to give information.

trade union   An organisation of workers in a trade or profession formed to protect their rights and to represent them in discussions with their employers, often to improve wages and working conditions.

trans-Atlantic   Crossing the Atlantic Ocean between Britain and the USA.

truce   An agreement between two groups or individuals to stop fighting for a short period of time.

upper-class   Belonging to the group of people in a society who have the highest social status.

viaduct   A long, high bridge, often a series of arches, carrying a road or railway across a valley.

Vikings   Scandinavian pirates and traders who attacked villages in north-western Europe from the 8th to the 11th centuries.

World Wide Web   A computer system on the internet that links documents and pictures into a database that people all over the world can use.

Zoroastrianism   A religion founded in Persia by the prophet Zoroaster in the 6th century BCE. Zoroastrians believe in one god, called Ahura Mazda, and are guided by the principle: good thoughts, good words, good deeds.

INDEX

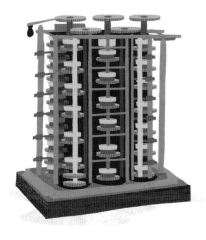

ACKNOWLEDGEMENTS

Nosy Crow would like to thank Rachel Faturoti, Miranda Baker and Jo Empson.

Imogen Russell Williams would like to thank Julia Gray for her Ada Lovelace expertise, Alastair Harper for historical help and copious tea, Dr Philip Abraham for astute and constructive criticism, Matthew Bergin for help with programming and black holes, and Elizabeth Jenner for ambitious, sensitive editing and continually pushing the book to be bigger and better.

Sara Mulvanny A special thanks to my wonderful partner Marc for never moaning when I have to work evenings and weekends. There are no words to express just how much I love and appreciate you.
I'm so grateful for all my family and friends for their love and encouragement, albeit from afar this last year.
I want to say a thank you to the Nosy Crow team for their hard work in making this book a reality.
And lastly a big thanks to my agent Helen at Agency Rush for her support and wisdom throughout the years.